THE PROFIT-BOOSTING PRINCIPLES

HOW TO DRAMATICALLY INCREASE YOUR
MARTIAL ARTS SCHOOL PROFITS WITHOUT
INCREASING YOUR OVERHEAD

MIKE MASSIE

MODERN DIGITAL PUBLISHING
AUSTIN, TEXAS

Modern Digital Publishing
P.O. Box 270132
Austin, TX 78727
www.MartialArtsBusinessDaily.com

Ordering Information:
Quantity sales. Special discounts are available on quantity purchases by cor-
porations, associations, and others. For details, contact the "Special Sales
Department" at the address above.

The Profit-Boosting Principles/ Mike Massie. —1st ed.
ISBN 978-0-9896683-1-6

Contents

Dedicated to Deanna and Caleb

"Profits are better than wages. Wages make you a living; profits make you a fortune."

-- Jim Rohn

Introduction

This book reveals how you can dramatically increase the profit margins in your martial arts school without significantly increasing your overhead, simply by applying three "Profit-Boosting Principles" in your studio operations. While this may seem like a bold claim, I can tell you with a certainty that it is possible to increase your net profit considerably using the methods described in this book.

However, I'd like to first point out that the martial arts business management techniques I share here are only one half of the profitability coin. The other half is in setting up your martial arts school so you have low overhead in the first place, a topic I deal with in great detail in *Small Dojo Big Profits*. If you are starting a martial arts school, or considering expanding your current operations and you have not yet read *Small Dojo Big Profits*, I strongly encourage you to do first before you start implementing the techniques and information in this book.

The reason is because without having set up your school first to be a lean and mean, low overhead, *Small Dojo Big Profits* school, no matter how much money you gross your net profits will suffer considerably. Not that the methods I describe here won't allow you to make more money in your studio; far from it. However, if your foundational profit margins are already low because your overhead is sky-high, you're going to be operating your business in direct violation of my most basic principles for running an SDBP school, which will mean that you're going to be working awfully hard for a lot less pay than you *could* be making.

Having said that, let me also say right up front that this book is not about raking your clients over the coals or squeezing them for all their worth. I am strongly against the sadly popular martial arts school management approach that advises you to get as much money up front as possible (because most students in the commercial schools that use this approach don't hang around longer than six months). To me, that's profiting off your own failures and shortcomings as an instructor. Inherently there's nothing wrong with getting paid up front, but when you're doing so in full knowledge of the fact that your average client drops out early because your service is horrible, there's an obvious ethical shortfall.

On the contrary, this book is really all about improving your students' experience and increasing the quality of the training you provide. In short, it's about providing increased value for your customers. That is most definitely the heart of this book, and it's also the heart of the *Small Dojo Big Profits* approach to starting and running a successful martial arts school. I fully believe that only by embracing this philosophy completely will you come to realize that financial success and running an ethical business are *not* mutually exclusive.

Ultimately, however, the responsibility to do so rests with you. I sincerely hope that as you read this book you gain a deeper understanding and a greater respect for the fact that, despite the lofty position we as martial arts instructors hold in our schools, ultimately we are in a *service* industry. While we are not subservient to our clients (ever), we do by the very nature of the student/teacher relationship serve our clientele. Once you begin to understand that you serve those you teach, you'll become a much more effective leader as you seek to improve the service you provide daily; and, that is when you'll be able to utilize what you learn in these pages most effectively.

- Mike Massie

[1]

First, How Honesty Can Really Make a Difference in Your Bottom Line

So, think you have some powerful "sales kung fu"? If so, you likely are aware that your customers see the enrollment process as a buying process. They are shopping you along with your competitors, and will probably make their buying decision based on how good you are at convincing them to join your school.

Having said that, you should know that I am not at all a fan of sneaky tricks and hard sell tactics. My advice is that you put away those slick tricks, because honesty and convenience are better than tricks, any day of the week. Allow me to present you with the number one rule I want you to live and die by in your sales process (and you will hear this again in this book):

> *"When you have the truth, you don't need tricks. Always tell the truth to your customers."*

No matter what you've been told, and no matter who told you to use them, slick tricks work against you and not for you when you are building your enrollment. Growing a school over the long-term is about building trust and a reputation for honesty in your community. Becoming known as the used car salesman among your local martial arts instructors is not the best way to achieve that goal.

Accordingly, I want you to adopt an approach that features honesty and common sense courtesy in order to increase your sales and conversions. In that regard, I don't think I need to go into detail with you about how to tell the truth to your customers. However, I would like to go over some of the most egregious "slick tricks" martial arts school owners have been taught to use with their customers, so you can see how stupid it makes you look when you use these tactics.

YOUR CUSTOMERS AREN'T STUPID, SO RESPECT THEIR INTELLIGENCE

Many of the selling tricks I've heard "martial arts business consultants" suggest over the years made me want to go shower just by hearing them. Here are a few doozies I've heard or been advised to use over the years:

- **"Your registration fee is for insurance."** – Huh? So, I'm to believe that it costs a business owner $299 to pay for insurance on a single customer? Give me a break...
- **"We can't cancel your membership. The billing company controls that. So, you'll have to call them to make any changes to your membership."** – Seriously? You have no control over how your customer accounts are handled?
- **"The billing company charges us a fee for each new student. That's why we have to charge you a registration fee."** Hmmm... your billing company charges you $300 to

process some paperwork? I'd say it's time to get a new billing company or to do that in-house, don't you think?

- **"It's been two weeks since you enrolled, and we believe your child has what it takes to become a Black Belt in this school. That's why we're offering you a special, one-time only discount on upgrading to our Black Belt Club membership."** – Really? After just two weeks you can tell that my child is ready to commit to four years of doing the same activity 3-4 times a week? Your powers of perception astonish me – will my child learn these same Jedi skills in your "Black Belt Club"?

- **"The testing fees are for your international certification of rank."** – So, my kid is going to be able to take his yellow belt to Kazakhstan and it'll be recognized there? Well, that's comforting...

- **"No, we don't use contracts. This silly little piece of paper here? Simply a formality."** – Well, in that case, let's just skip that formality entirely, shall we?

Can you see how obvious the con is in each instance? Believe me, the majority of your customers will, too. And, even if they go along with it, you will lose a considerable amount of their respect by using these cons on them.

Bottom line? Just tell the truth! I can assure you, no one ever lost any respect by telling the truth to their customers. Your customers will appreciate it, and they'll be a lot more loyal to you in the long run as a result as well.

- - -

Now, let's look at the specific ways you can increase your profits without significantly increasing your overhead.

[2]

How to Increase Your Martial Arts School Profits Without Increasing Your Overhead

In Jay Abraham's excellent book, *Getting Everything You Can Out of All You've Got*, Mr. Abraham states that there are only three ways you can increase your business:

1. By increasing your number of clients –
2. By increasing the average size of the sale per client –
3. By increasing the number of times clients return and buy again.

In truth, this is no great revelation. Every savvy business owner knows that these three areas of focus are where the real profits are in a small business. In fact, I learned this very thing when I was studying business at university.

But the thing is, knowing something is true in business as opposed to knowing how to apply that knowledge in practical terms can make all the difference between failure and success. Out of necessity, I learned the practical application of these principles long before I ever attended a single college business course. In fact, it was only later when I learned these principles in college and read Mr. Abraham's book that I realized how I had applied those very principles to achieve financial success in my own studios.

So, let's take a look at these three "Profit-Boosting Principles" in order to see how exactly we can apply them to the business of teaching martial arts.

Profit-Boosting Principle #1: Increasing Your Number of Clients

Obviously, increasing your client base is the sole and immediate purpose of all the marketing you do. However, there are some very simple means of doing this that school owners often overlook. These methods will cost you little in time or expense to implement, but can have a significant impact on your enrollment.

Yes, there are simple low-cost ways of getting new clients. However, the sad fact is that most business owners only focus on that one aspect of increasing their number of customers, that being marketing to get new clients. As you'll see later in this book, that very poor application of this profit-boosting principle can actually end up hurting your school in the long run by limiting your growth. I know that sounds contradictory, but hold that thought until later when I explain the dynamics of growing the enrollment numbers in your martial arts school.

Profit-Boosting Principle #2: Increasing the Average Size of the Sale

Wouldn't it be nice if you could make twice as much profit every single time you enrolled a new student? Of course it would, but I already know what you're thinking. "I can't gouge my customers like that, blah, blah, blah."

Well, here's a thought... what if you actually provided more value to the new student at the time of their enrollment, thereby providing them with something that they will want to pay more for up front? Pay attention here, because this principle of providing value actually resides at the center of everything I'm about to reveal to you in this book.

It's only by providing more value that you will be able to ethically increase your profits in your business. Remember that; write it down backwards and paste it to your forward if you have to, because it's that important.

PROFIT-BOOSTING PRINCIPLE #3: INCREASING THE FREQUENCY OF THE SALE

Increasing the number of times clients buy may seem difficult when you run a business that is based on monthly payments. However, there are plenty of ways to get your students to buy more often. I used to think that the only way to generate profit in a martial arts school was by selling more memberships, but I was mistaken. Actually, there are dozens of ways to generate income in your studio; that's right, I said dozens.

The thing is, you have to be of a mindset that allows you to spot ways of providing increased value to your students. Again, it's only by adding value that you can ethically increase your profits. Once you adopt the attitude of adding value at every opportunity, you'll be well on your way to finding ways to increase the number of times your clients pull out their credit cards and checkbooks in your school.

THE DESIRED OUTCOME

In this book I'm going to show you how to apply these principles to your martial arts school business operations in order to dramatically increase your profits. And just how "dramatic" will that profit increase be? How's an 80% or greater increase in net profits sound? I think you'll agree, that's a tune any martial arts school owner can dance to... and that's exactly what I'm going to show you in this manual.

But, just one thing before we get started... I need you to keep an open mind. That's because some of the ideas I present in this book have been considered controversial by many in the martial arts industry. However, I'm going to show you how these methods have been abused by other instructors and schools over time. Then, I'm going to show you how to use them ethically and in a manner that's completely in line with your moral standards.

Are you ready to learn how to dramatically boost your martial arts business profits? Then let's get started...

[3]

Principle #1

Increasing Your Number of Clients

I've said many times that when you're in business, *you're in the business of attracting new business.* Well, that's very true, but you're also in the business of keeping your customers. And, in the martial arts instruction business, the responsibility of keeping customers around is exceptionally important, as you'll discover on the following pages.

> **True story:** *Several years ago, I ran a promotion on my private business coaching forum to encourage my forum members to enroll as many students as possible in a three-month period. One school owner who had previously been struggling to get new students took everything I told him to do, and he did it; I mean, he did everything I told them to do to get new students.*
>
> *The first thing on the list was hiring me to revamp his website. Then, he went to work on the list of marketing action steps I provided to all the forum members at the time. And, it worked. He ended up enrolling over 100 students in 120 days... and that's where the problems started.*
>
> *See, this school owner hadn't paid attention to what I teach about retention strategies, and as it turns out his retention was less than 40%; meaning, out of those 100 students he enrolled, he only kept about 40 of them around for longer than six months. (In fact, I only found out about this from another instructor*

that he'd confided in, because he was too ashamed to tell me after we'd made such a big deal out of his success in using my marketing system.)

Also, what he found was that he couldn't keep bringing in that many new students while still keeping his existing students happy. I mean, it's great to bring in 25 students a month, but you have to have retention strategies in place in order to keep them and to keep your existing students happy while you're taking care of all those new students. So, he also ended up losing a great deal of his existing students as well. In fact, at the end of a year, he was right back where he started.

My point is that it wasn't anything that this school owner did to chase away all those students; it's what he didn't do that caused them to leave. The sad thing is I could have easily shown him what he had to do to keep those students around, if he'd only shared with me that he was having retention challenges. And, that's the whole point of this story...

While I cover all the steps I told him to take to get those 100 students in 120 days in my Martial Arts Marketing Success System, what I'm about to cover in this book will explain not only how important it is to keep those students around, but also precisely how you're going to keep them around. And as you'll see, there's no way to grow a martial arts school unless you maintain a high level of customer satisfaction in order to keep your retention high.

Key Point: Marketing is only one-half of the martial arts school growth equation; the other half is retention, and I'd say it's even more important than marketing to your school's growth.

So, pay very close attention to exactly the action steps I recommend you take in order to keep your students happy and your retention high. By doing so, and so long as you're marketing your martial arts school effectively, you'll see a steady increase in your enrollment numbers over time and you'll also maintain a healthy, sustainable growth curve in your school as well. Now, let's start by getting more specific about why retention is so important to your school's growth.

ONCE YOU FILL YOUR SCHOOL, YOU HAVE TO WORK TO KEEP IT FULL

As I've said many times on my blog and in my books, when you're starting a new martial art school (or any business) your first priority is building revenue. Cash flow is what runs a business and what keeps it running. Without cash flow your business simply will not grow.

Now, building cash flow is a function of marketing and sales. We market to attract new prospective clients, and then use effective sales tactics to enroll them in our programs. Simple, right?

However, as I mentioned previously the thing many school owners overlook are retention systems. Retention systems allow you to keep the cash flow that you have, so you aren't spinning your wheels by taking one step forward and two steps back in growing your school.

I've seen this happen many times with new school owners as well as with experienced but under-performing school owners who begin implementing my recommended marketing practices in their business. If they don't have quality-control and retention systems in place to handle the sudden influx of students, they'll have a very hard time keeping those students they worked so very hard to get, and that's a crying shame.

Let me just say that enrolling 50 or 100 new students in a few months, and then having to deal with the subsequent customer service and retention issues... well, this is a good problem to have. However, if you don't have systems in place to handle rapid growth, you will lose those students and never reap the financial rewards of owning a healthy thriving school.

Not only that, but retention becomes critical once you hit the 100 student mark in your school. If you fail to implement successful and effective retention strategies, your school's growth will stall at this stage. For a mathematical illustration of why this occurs (as well as an introduction to retention systems), let's examine how this plays out in most martial arts schools.

A Practical Illustration of the Importance of Retention Strategies

Or, "Treading Water" in Your Martial Arts Business

When you are first starting your school, building your revenues through marketing and recruitment is your first and foremost priority. Due to the fact that your overall enrollment numbers are relatively low, retention is not an issue at this early stage in the game. That's why, before you hit the 50-100 student mark, you can almost completely focus on marketing and recruiting new students.

Why Retention Becomes So Important After Your First Year

However, as time goes on your enrollment numbers will increase, thereby making retention an increasing concern for your school's growth after your first or second year in business.

Here's why...

For example, let's just say hypothetically that you opened your doors with 40 students that you had from your part-time programs, and you enrolled another 20 in the first month during your grand opening, with your initial marketing and publicity push, and by holding open house bring-a-friend events for all your classes.

So, starting with an enrollment of 60 students, let's say that you are able to enroll ten new students a month, based on:

- 20 leads per month,
- With 80 percent setting an appointment for their first intro lesson (16 left),

- 80 percent of those attending their first intro lesson (13 left),
- And 80 percent of those students enrolling on a regular membership (about 10 total enrollments).

Now, let's also say that you are able to keep your attrition (dropout) rate down to 5 percent a month, which is at the top end of the industry standard (lower is better, so 5 percent is kind of high).

SOME ENROLLMENT PROJECTIONS FOR YOU TO CONSIDER...

Calculating your enrollment numbers for your first year, **this is what your enrollment will look like over the course of your first 12 months in business:**

Month	1	2	3	4	5	6	7	8	9	10	11	12
New members	60	10	10	10	10	10	10	10	10	10	10	10
Drop outs (5%)	3	3	4	4	4	5	5	5	5	6	6	6
Total enrolled	57	64	70	76	82	87	92	97	102	106	110	114

And at the end of 2 years:

Month	13	14	15	16	17	18	19	20	21	22	23	24
New members	10	10	10	10	10	10	10	10	10	10	10	10
Drop outs (5%)	6	6	7	7	7	7	7	7	7	8	8	8
Total enrolled	118	122	125	128	131	134	137	140	143	145	147	149

Now, as you can see from these numbers, your margin for error gets increasingly narrower as time goes on, due to your attrition (drop out) rate remaining a constant at 5 percent attrition...

This is because of the fact that your total number of drop outs each month keeps climbing (based on 5 percent of your total enrollment) while your number of new enrollments stays the same.

And at the end of three years, should you continue to maintain these numbers:

Month	25	26	27	28	29	30	31	32	33	34	35	36
New members	10	10	10	10	10	10	10	10	10	10	10	10
Drop outs (5%)	8	8	8	8	8	8	8	8	8	8	9	9
Total enrolled	151	153	155	157	159	161	163	165	167	169	170	171

TOPPING OUT AND STAGNATING: WITHOUT RETENTION STRATEGIES, IT'S A CERTAINTY

At this point, it is true that you'll be running a successful small school, assuming that you've followed the *Small Dojo Big Profits* method and kept your overhead low and your profit margins high.

However, if your retention hasn't improved, your growth will now stagnate and stall. Furthermore, *your margin for error is quite narrow* when it comes to maintaining your enrollment numbers. Should you have a particularly poor month (traditionally, July and August during the summer, and November/December during fall and winter), your enrollment may actually decline temporarily, and you'll find yourself taking one step forward and two steps back.

This is why you must have retention strategies in place by the end of your first year in business (and preferably earlier) to decrease your drop outs and increase your retention. Something else to consider... if your goal is to graduate black belts who can eventually teach for you to take some of the load off your back, you'll rarely see anyone stick around long enough to get their black belt if your attrition rate remains at 5 percent a month.

That's because at 5% attrition you'll be losing approximately 50% of a given group of students each year. So, of that group of 10 students that you enroll this month, hypothetically only 5 will be around next year, and only a few will be around the following year. I know this is fuzzy math, but in reality the numbers do work out this way over time.

This is why so many schools offer Black Belt Club memberships, to entice students to enroll for the long haul and commit to staying for 2 or even 3 years. It's also why so many studios are turning to cash outs. They'd rather get their money up front because they know they'll make more money that way, versus allowing students to pay it over time when they may drop out after 6 months or so. (Again, in my opinion this is profiting from failure, because I believe that if you can't keep the majority of your students around longer than six months you need to consider finding another vocation.)

So, now that you understand the importance of retention systems, let's take a close look at how you're going to keep those students.

[4]

Why the Real Profit Is In the Follow-Up

It's often been said in sales that the real profit is in the follow-up. And that's why during the enrollment process when a student is initially checking out our school on a "trial" or introductory membership, we tend to be high-touch because we're still in the courting stage with the prospective student. We may call to follow-up with the student, send a thank you card or a personal note to welcome them to the school, and take extra time to chat with them before or after class.

But let me ask you... what typically happens after that student enrolls? Let's be honest; after the student enrolls much of that extra attention stops, and often nearly completely. This leaves the new student feeling like they're just a paycheck and not a person.

If you treat your students this way, pretty soon they're going to start to talk. And what they'll talk about is how you only spend time with the new students, and how you never have time for people once they enroll. This is bad juju, folks. So remember, it's what you do *after* the student enrolls that counts most toward your long-term success. And that's exactly where implementing retention strategies comes into play for increasing your number of clients (Profit-Boosting Principle #1).

Quantitative Retention Strategies

Quantitative retention strategies consist of concrete actions that can provide a directly measurable increase in your active enrollment numbers. In other words, you do retention strategy "A", and you get a measurable increase in your enrollment numbers for the following period that you can directly attribute to using that strategy.

I suggest that you don't experiment with these one at a time, but instead that you implement them all at once. The reason is that singly they may not make that much of an impact, but cumulatively they will make a huge difference in your retention. So without further ado, here are three tried-and-true quantitative retention strategies you can implement in your school.

Auto-Renewal Clauses

If your state allows it, include an auto-renewal clause in your membership agreement. This is simply a clause that states the membership will be automatically renewed at the end of the term, unless the customer gives you a written notice 30 days prior to the end of the initial term. (Note: Make sure you explain this clearly when you enroll new students.)

The benefit to the student is that their tuition is locked in... even if you increase your tuition rates next year, they'll continue to pay the same tuition for so long as they keep their membership. Basically, fear of loss is used as an enticement for your students to stay enrolled. And the benefit to you is that you don't have to continue chasing down students to renew their memberships, a significant time-saver in my experience.

And, this can help to boost your retention numbers considerably as well. The reason? *It places the onus for leaving on the client, instead of placing the responsibility on you for keeping them enrolled.* Although it may only increase your renewals incrementally, by using auto renewals you could see your attrition drop from 5 percent to 4.5 or even 4 percent; every little bit counts.

EXTENDED MEMBERSHIP AND DISCOUNT OPTIONS

Offering discounts for longer-term enrollment periods is another method to increase retention. I do this by offering what amounts to a free month of tuition for each 12 months a student extends their membership (spread out over the entire payment term), which is just one approach to using this method.

Many students will see the benefit to enrolling for a longer period, knowing that they will be making lower monthly payments and saving more over the long haul. So, they'll be likewise enticed to enroll and commit for a longer period. However, this ultimately decreases your tuition collections, but it's a fair trade-off for the increased enrollment numbers.

In fact your goal should be to get 100% of your students enrolled on extended memberships. Ideally you want to do this without collecting less tuition overall, which many schools have been able to do by using other retention strategies. Read on to find out what I've found to be the best way to make this happen.

OFFERING EXTENDED ADDED-VALUE MEMBERSHIPS

Offering additional services bundled with extended-length memberships has long been another viable retention method for martial arts schools. Typically, this is what most schools refer to as their "Black Belt Club". A common approach is to offer additional classes (we offer one additional class per week) and special privileges for students who commit to training for a longer period of time (2 – 3 years). Tuition is generally higher for these programs, perhaps 25 to 50 percent higher than the basic tuition rate.

However, by making these students feel "special" (via recognition, making it a pre-qualification for demo teams and competition, and increased opportunities for advancement) you would be surprised how many students would jump at the opportunity to be part of an elite group within your school. I'll go into more detail about how you can utilize this strategy ethically in the next chapter, but for now just understand that in an SDBP school, so-called Black Belt Club programs are about providing extra training, not selling belts.

QUALITATIVE RETENTION STRATEGIES

These are things that can't be measured that still have a definite impact on your retention. I saved these for last, because I wanted you to look at quantitative methods before we discussed qualitative methods for increasing retention. The reason is simple; just as it's much more important that you focus on increasing your revenue when you first launch your business, it is also more important that you *first* focus on measurable methods of improving your retention that provide concrete, measurable feedback in the way of improved retention numbers. This is for no other reason than to get you to start thinking in hard numbers, because that's ultimately going to be the path to your long-term success in managing your studio.

However, while it's better at first to start thinking in terms of concrete methods for increasing retention such as those discussed above, it is often more effective as an overall retention solution to simply improve the quality of service and instruction in your school. So, here are a few simple retention strategies you can implement that focus on improving the quality of your programs, as well as the customer experience for your clients.

IMPROVED CUSTOMER SERVICE

Going that extra mile can go a long way toward making your customers feel wanted. And, making your students feel wanted is as important to your retention as water is to soup. It's long been accepted that "perceived instructor indifference" is a major cause of student dropouts, so by letting our students know that we care, we can prevent student attrition rates from getting too high.

Now, don't get confused; you certainly don't want to "spoil" your students. Many instructors have made the mistake of trying to cater to their students' every whim and fancy, and ended up stressed out and frustrated once they realized their students lost respect for them as an authority figure. Think about how spoiled kids who get whatever they want don't respect their parents – you'll get a similar result if you start jumping through hoops to please your students.

The point is not to cater to them, but instead to make them feel wanted; there's a subtle but important difference here. That's why many schools use phone calls and personal mail correspondence to increase retention among their students.

Examples:
1. **Calling new students** as a courtesy after 2 weeks, 4 weeks, and 6 weeks of enrollment;
2. **Sending a personal "welcome" note to all new students** the week that they enroll;
3. **Sending birthday cards;**
4. **Calling all students who missed classes** on Monday and Tuesday that Wednesday, and calling all students who missed classes on Wednesday and Thursday that Friday;
5. **Sending MIA *"We Missed You in Class!"* cards** to all students who missed classes for a full week.

Teaching Better Classes

Finally, simply improving the quality of your instruction can go a long way to keeping students in class. Learning better teaching methods that improve your ability to transmit knowledge is one way to do this. Start by studying learning styles and how people learn new things. I suggest that you read my other books, *Character Education Lesson Plans for Children* and *Developing Staff and Leadership Teams* for more on this topic (both are available at Amazon.com).

Organizing Your Curriculum into Manageable Steps and Achievable Goals

In addition, consider having a set curriculum that makes achieving a black belt attainable, while keeping it a prestigious and worthy goal. The way to do this is to break your curriculum down in steps, based on rank levels and experience.

For example:

- **Beginners** – White, Yellow
- **Intermediate** – Green, Blue
- **Advanced** – Red, Brown
- **Black Belt** – 1st Degree, 2nd Degree, etc.

Also, I strongly suggest that you set up your entire curriculum from white belt to black belt as a rotating curriculum. You can read my book, *How to Teach Martial Arts Using a Rotating Curriculum*, for more information on this.

- - -

I hope this helps you understand not only the importance of having good retention strategies in place during the second year of your school's growth, but also how to implement those strategies. I encourage you to implement one new strategy a month as you work on increasing your retention. Finally, keep it simple by focusing on easy to implement tasks that you are able to manage without adding too much extra work to your schedule. Now, let's examine a few of these easy-to-implement retention strategies and look at how to implement them.

[5]

Retention Systems

CARING AS A RETENTION STRATEGY

Sure, you care about your students... but do they know it? You may not realize this, but retention is a whole lot easier when you invest time in letting your students *know* that you care about them, both personally and as martial arts students. Showing students (and parents) that you care can go a long way toward keeping them around for the long haul.

Let me be the first to admit that martial arts instructors tend to not be the most sensitive people in the world. Admit it – you probably don't often express your feelings toward others, and usually just expect that your feelings are "understood." Well, unless you're teaching jedi knights and X-men (empaths and mind readers, in case you're not a sci-fi junkie like me), chances are good that no one in your school is quite sure whether or not you really care about them, personally, or otherwise.

And, even if you don't find it difficult to express that you care about other people, you may not even be communicating it in a way they can understand. Often, people have different ways of showing and interpreting appreciation (as any married couple can attest). So, finding ways to make certain you get the message across to your students is a prerequisite to having good relationships with your students.

Don't Sweat It – It's Easier than You May Think

Communicating that you care about your students really isn't all that difficult or complex. All it takes is a little awareness and a few extra minutes invested each day in communicating with your students. Here are a few simple action steps you can take to make sure your students (and parents) know that you are personally invested in their well-being:

1. **Personal notes** – Birthday cards, good job notes and MIA notes have long been a standard retention tool in our industry. But how many of us actually take the time to jot a quick, personal, hand-written note every so often just to check in on a student? If you think about it, just by writing two notes a day five days a week, you'll personally connect with 100 students over the course of 10 weeks. And, the impact this can have on your school is phenomenal. Make it a daily habit and see what it can do for your students.

2. **Emails and texts** – Similar to the above, but for the wired generation. Think about this... lots of kids have their own cell phones these days, and use texting more than any other mode of communication. How cool would it be if you were a kid, and your karate instructor sent you a text that said, "Hi John, just wanted to tell you that your kicks are really looking great. Keep up the good work!" Do you think that kid's attitude would suddenly soar? Of course it would!

3. **Greet every student by name** – The sweetest words in the English language usually begin with hearing your own name. Show you care by caring enough to greet every student with a smile, by name, every day.

4. **Pre- and post-class chats** – Just saying hi and greeting students is a good start... but how about making it a habit to answer questions after every class? Set aside five or ten minutes after each class for "question time." It means a lot to kids when you take time to hear about their latest story or life event; it doesn't take much to be a person who matters in their life! Adults may also appreciate the opportunity to get specific technical questions answered, and parents like to connect with people who are influencing their kids. Be accessible and it will endear you to your students for life.

5. **Recognition and awards** – At least once every quarter, recognize someone who has done something outstanding in your school. And, once a year hold an awards dinner to recognize the students and staff in your school who so richly deserve your praise. These events mean a lot to your students, and they are excellent opportunities to bond as a school as well.

To some of you, the above steps may seem obvious. But, it's often the obvious that gets overlooked. I challenge you to measure your current retention averages, and then to make it a habit to implement the above actions in your school regularly. After three months, compare your previous and current retention numbers and you'll be amazed at the differences.

YOUR BUILT-IN RETENTION PROGRAM

HOW TO SET UP AND PROMOTE A BLACK BELT CLUB PROGRAM IN YOUR SCHOOL

While black belt is the pinnacle of achievement for most students, Black Belt Club can be a way to provide your most dedicated students with additional training opportunities and at the same time improve your student retention. While some schools are resistant to the idea of having an elite membership in their studio, the fact remains that many of your students will jump at the chance to belong to such a program.

The reason is that you already have students who are extremely dedicated and motivated to train... so why not offer them a program that recognizes and rewards them for their commitment? Black Belt Club is a perfect way to do this.

And, before you get worked up into a tizzy about selling belts, let me clarify by saying that the way I set up my BBC has nothing to do with selling belts. Instead, it's all about keeping the program quality high and rewarding good students. Here's how I do it...

How I Set-Up and Promote My BBC

In my schools, BBC is a special once a week class that covers something the students don't normally get to do in their regular classes. For example, in my first school the curriculum basically followed a set of weapons DVDs by a popular instructor. I attended a seminar on those forms that was taught by this person, and I liked the forms so much that I bought his DVDs and started teaching them to my BBC as follows:

- The kids got to do a new weapon every 1-2 months...
- Changing weapons each month increased Pro Shop sales...
- And everyone was happy...

The point is that you don't have to have a complicated curriculum set up to have a successful BBC program. Just choose curricula and activities that will be popular among your students and that will make them better black belts.

Promoting Is Easier When You Advertise Properly (And Use the Velvet Rope)

I purposely schedule my BBC classes right before or after one of our most popular classes, which is a sparring class that is required of green belts and above. That's so the other kids will see the BBC kids with their weapons.

I think you can figure out the rest.

Now, here's the kicker – you can't just "sign-up" for BBC in my schools. Oh no...

I require my students to have at least 6 months experience and be at the second belt in our system, and they have to have good grades, good attendance in class, and a good attitude at the martial arts school, at home, and at school. Then, they have to apply to join. That's right – they have to write me a letter in their own words about why they want to join.

And, I do actually turn some students away if I think they don't have the qualifications I'm looking for in my BBC members. I've even kicked some kids out in the past. However, I always provide a clear path and expectations to get in (or get back in if they are kicked out). People always want what they can't have, folks. This serves to make demand high and to keep your program quality high as well.

WHAT TO OFFER YOUR BBC MEMBERS – THE "EXTRAS"

BBC members are often offered "perks" that sweeten the deal and add value to their membership. The benefits you offer will depend on what your "regular" members already get (in my schools, all regular members get is two classes a week). Here are some ideas I pulled out of some sales copy I wrote for a well-known instructor not too long ago:

- Discounts on school-sponsored special events...
- A special weekly class for Black Belt Club members only...
- Tuition rates locked in until the student earns their black belt...
- A free private lesson every month...
- Free belt exams...
- Special Black Belt Club patch...

- Special Black Belt Club belt...
- Special BBC uniform...
- Etc...

I bet you can come up with more – that's just to give you ideas. Be creative, add value, but make sure you can deliver on whatever you offer.

What to Charge for BBC

I suggest you offer three standard program and pricing levels in your school; a basic membership, a "mid-level membership", and BBC. I recommend charging 20% over your base price for the mid-level, and up to 50% more for BBC.

Now, there's only one base price for BBC, but students should be able to join for 2, 3, or 4 years, with each additional time commitment giving them a bit of a discount over the regular price. But, the minimum commitment for BBC is two years. That's so you only get committed and dedicated students in your BBC. Remember, BBC is NOT for wimps, it's for the most dedicated students in the school. (Repeat after me – "NO EASY BLACK BELTS!")

BBC Recap

Just to recap what we covered in this chapter:

- BBC is for rewarding students and improving retention among your most dedicated students...
- The curriculum doesn't have to be complicated, only something fun, different, and beneficial to the students...
- BBC is NOT an "everyone can come" program – use the Velvet Rope and keep the quality high...
- Offer lots of "extras" for your BBC members (more recognition)

- Charge about 50% more for BBC membership, and require a longer-term commitment to join.

Above all though, have fun implementing your BBC program. It's a great way to offer added value, and also a great opportunity for bonding with your most loyal and dedicated students. Used ethically, your BBC will become the strong core of your martial arts school, and it will provide you and your students with rewarding experiences for years to come.

Oh, I forgot to mention the "hidden added bonus" for running a BBC program. So what's this hidden added bonus of running a BBC program in your school? It's the fact that these students often become your best candidates for employment later on down the road when it's time to hire staff for your school. (Note: For even more information on this you can read my book on the topic, *Developing Staff and Leadership Teams*, available at Amazon.com.)

Using Paper to Increase Retention

Changing the Relationship Dynamic between You and Your Students by Using Membership Agreements

Many instructors ask me, "Why use membership agreements?" My response is, *"Why **not** use them?"* This seems to be an age-old controversy among martial art school owners, and it's one that bears examining.

First, let's discuss why there's so much controversy surrounding the use of membership agreements in the first place. If you're against using membership agreements, I'll bet it's because of one of the following three reasons:

- You've seen them used unethically in the past,
- You've seen them used ineffectively in the past,
- You've seen them used inconsistently in the past.

Well, I'm about to shatter those preconceptions by showing you not only why they're so important to your school's financial success, but also how to use them ethically as well.

CAN YOU RUN A SUCCESSFUL SCHOOL WITHOUT USING CONTRACTS?

Everyone wants to know this, and here's my honest answer after running schools for over twenty years and speaking to literally hundreds of school owners:

In a word, "no."

Now, I know there are schools out there that say they don't use them and they have X-hundred number of students. I say bull malarkey. Maybe they do have that many students at a given time of the year, and maybe they don't. However, they have to be doing some pretty extraordinary things to keep a large school going without using membership agreements.

- Number one, they need to have an extraordinarily good retention system in place.
- Number two, they have to have an incredible marketing system in place to replace all the students coming and going all the time.
- And number three, they better have a ton of money put aside in the bank to pay the bills when everyone cancels in November and May each year.

See, no matter how "dedicated" students say they are, when given a choice they aren't going to pay for something they aren't using. During the slower summer and winter months when attendance is low, when given a choice students who aren't coming to your classes will stop paying. Also, people spend their disposable income based on their present priorities. When it comes between paying for lessons and having a big Christmas, or paying for lessons and going to Disneyland, which do you think mom and dad will choose?

WHY YOU MUST USE MEMBERSHIP AGREEMENTS

REASON #1 – INCOME STABILIZATION

For one, they stabilize your income. Your bills are the same whether Charlie or Jenny or Mickey or Joey show up for class or not. You have to pay your rent, your light bill, and your salary each and every month, month in and month out, regardless of who attends your classes. This is your livelihood, for goodness sakes. You MUST take it seriously, and that means forcing your students to do so, too.

So instead of having students come and go as they wish, using membership agreements forces them to make a financial commitment to your school. And that means you can continue to teach professionally and give 100% of your time and energy to your students, instead of giving them what's left over after your day job at Spacely Sprockets, Initech, or Dunder Mifflin.

REASON #2 – LIMITED TIME, SPACE, AND CLASSES

Speaking of which, how many instructors want to spend their time with wishy-washy students? I don't know about you, but I have limited time to teach, a limited amount of classes, a limited amount of space on my floor, and therefore I have to limit how many people I spend that time, space, and those class slots on.

I sure can't afford to give them to wishy-washy, "here today and gone tomorrow" students. I really prefer to spend my time working with students that are serious. So, by making them agree to commit to a certain length of training, I weed out the non-serious students.

Reason #3 – Chuck Norris Was Not Built In a Day

In addition, learning martial arts is a time-intensive activity. It takes time to learn what I teach; it can't be learned correctly in a few weeks or months. Therefore, I feel it's necessary to explain this to new students, so they have realistic expectations about their training.

Furthermore, it follows that I won't take money from someone who expects otherwise. If they can't make a time commitment to learning martial arts, I see no reason to take their money or to waste my time on them.

Remember, beginners are the hardest students to teach, and require much more of your time and effort than your existing students. I choose to spend that time and effort only on serious students. If they don't like it, they can find another place to train.

So, How Do You "Sell" It?

Again, use the truth. *"When you have the truth, you don't need tricks."*

Simply explaining the reasons for using membership agreements that I described above to new students greatly smoothes out the enrollment process. Most students are happy to make a commitment to your school, once they realize you are as serious about their progress and success as you are about their commitment to learn.

Also, make sure you make the terms of your membership clear. I allow anyone to cancel at any time for any reason within the first 30 days of their membership. That's because I want them to be absolutely certain that my school is the place they want to train at. If they can't make a decision in 30 days, they need to go train somewhere else.

I explain that my membership agreement is just like their gym membership; regardless of whether they show up to class or not, they still have to pay their tuition. So, if for any reason they decide it's not for them within the first 30 days, they need to let me know; after the

31st day they will be expected to pay regardless of whether or not they use their membership.

Did you catch the language there? I put it on them, not on me. *It's their choice whether they show up to train or not.*

Just be honest and up front about your reasons for making students commit, and most people will understand. Those that don't probably wouldn't be the best students anyway. Believe me; using contracts ethically will go a long way toward improving your school and increasing your income.

[6]

More Easy Ways to Boost Your Enrollment

Besides working on your retention, there are a few more very simple ways you can increase you student enrollment without increasing your overhead. And while these are all marketing-related, they consist of doing some very simple things that can have dramatic results on increasing your enrollment.

Four Incredibly Easy Ways to Increase Your Student Enrollment

Offering Family Rates

By offering family rates, you can both increase the number of your clients, and increase the average size of the sale. While you may look at a single family as a single client, every member of that family that is not training at your school is a client you don't have. Make it clear you offer a discount for additional family members who want to join, and encourage your current students to invite other family members to try classes.

I offer 20% off for the second family member, 30% off for the third, 40% for the fourth, and so on. However, I really don't recommend that you have a "whole family" rate. Why? You might end up with the Duggar family in your school (this really happened to a school owner I know).

Putting Your Sales Presentation Online

You can only talk to one person at a time. Your website, on the other hand, can talk to an unlimited number of people 24 hours a day, 365 days a year. Create a video presentation of your programs and instructions on how to get started, and put it on the front page of your site with a lead capture form and special offer, ASAP.

Reactivating Old Students

Send a letter, use a text or email broadcast, or call them one at a time. Make each letter personal by addressing it personally to the inactive member. Here's an example:

Dear Mike,

It's been months since we've seen you here at Massie's Martial Arts. We miss you! Things have changed a lot since you've been gone. We've added some new classes, and we've also made it easier for you to come back in and start training again.

Right now, we're offering a 25% discount and no registration fee for any former member who wants to get back into training. So, there's never been a better time to start working toward your Black Belt again.

I hope to see you in class soon!

Sincerely,

Mr. Massie

P.S. - Stop by anytime for a free, no-obligation "we want you back" workout. I'd love to see you and find out what you've been up to.

Send a letter like this out to your inactive members monthly and see what happens.

Using Guest Passes

Use them. They're cheap, easy to implement, and effective, which is why I'm going to go into more detail on how to use them on the following pages.

How to Use Referral Programs to Attract New Students into Your Martial Arts School

After operating various martial arts schools and studios for two over decades, one thing that I have learned is that my students are my best advertisement. What I mean to say by that is that I get more people that call or stop by to join classes who say they heard about us from "a friend" than I generally get from paid advertisements.

That tells me that my students say positive things about my schools (which really makes me happy). And, if you are offering a quality program and treating your students right, you'll likely get quite a bit of new students from referrals as well.

In fact, referrals can end up being your number one source of new students. And once you start getting them, you don't want them to stop! So, in order to encourage referrals, it's a very good idea to offer a referral incentive program in your studio. We've used one for years that has worked very well for us, as I know it will for you.

Guest Pass Marketing

Using guest passes is a great way to increase referrals. The idea is that you make it easy for your members to refer their friends; you make them look like a hero to their friends when they do, and you reward them for doing so. It's a win-win all the way around.

Your guest passes (sometimes called "VIP cards") should be an ad for your school; if it looks like it's just a business card, it will be ineffective. For starters, it should actually say it's a FREE pass. Design it so when someone looks at it on either side, they instantly recognize it's good for a free class, a free week, two weeks free, or a month free at your school.

Also, if there's no value on the card, it will appear to be just another business card - and therefore worthless to anyone who receives it. Make sure you put the actual value of the pass on the front and back of the card. This will ensure that the majority of the people who receive it will either use it immediately, or keep it to give to a friend or for future use.

Boosting Response

The thing is, just saying it's good for "X" dollars worth of free lessons isn't enough. You actually have to TELL the person reading it what to do to redeem it. Give them explicit instructions at the end of the card – this is known as the "call to action" in marketing and advertising.

Also, give the recipient of the card multiple ways to contact you to redeem it. People are busy. If they think they have to actually go to your school to redeem it, they may decide it's too much trouble. So, provide them with all your contact info on the card... school name, address, phone number, website address, and email address.

I've said many times in the past that you need to get a short, easy-to-remember domain name (website address) to use in your ads. This is a perfect example of why you need one; the limited space on the guest pass is not conducive to including a long domain name. So, make sure you put your shortest domain name on your cards; it'll save space and make it easier to remember. Use one of the domains you have forwarded to your main website, one that is short, easy to remember, and that has to do with kids or that is fairly generic (or specific to your primary market).

So, the front of the card should say:

VIP GUEST PASS!

This card is good for one FREE month of classes at
ABC Martial Arts
Retail Value of over $100.00
Call 555-5555 to redeem and schedule your first FREE class!
Anytown Karate – 100 E. Main St. – Anytown, TX
www.YourTownKidsKarate.com – info@anytownkarate.com

INCREASING DISTRIBUTION

Now, let's talk about how to get your students to hand them out. We all know about referral incentive programs, but you need to get your students involved in the process. So, make sure you have a place for the student to put their own name on the back of the card – that way they know that *you'll* know who referred that student.

So, what the back of the card should say is:

FREE Guest Pass For: _____

Guest Referred by: _____

That leaves a lot of empty space back there though, doesn't it? Never waste space on an ad; ALWAYS use the back side of any business card, take one, door hanger, brochure, etc.

ADDING THAT EXTRA SOMETHING...

Now if you really want to make your VIP Guest Passes more effective, you can use the back space to sell your programs too. For example, you could get a domain name like "www.ProofKarateWorks.com" and forward it to your testimonials page, then put that on the back:

FREE Guest Pass For: _____

Guest Referred by: _____

Want to know why we're the best school in the Anytown area?
Visit www.ProofKarateWorks.com to hear what our students say!

It's outrageous, sure... but stuff like that works!

Also, be aware of the images you use on your VIP cards and ads. Kids with their arms crossed or that look too aggressive or harsh? No good. It will make them look like they have an attitude. Only use pictures with happy, smiling kids, or kids that are a "cute score of 10" on the mom scale (ten being any mom that saw the picture would go "aw, she's *soooo* cute").

GETTING THEM OUT THE DOOR

It's one thing to have them, but it's another to get your students handing them out. Here's how to get your students handing out these guest passes to increase your referrals:

- **Print up some nice looking business card size "Guest Passes"** and make them available to all students and staff. These cards should be good for one FREE MONTH of martial arts classes.

- **Tell your students to write their name on the back of every card** they hand out, and to give the "VIP" cards to whomever they wish.

- **Note: It's very important to be sure that only students and staff have access to your Guest Passes.** This elevates the value of the Guest Pass, since prospects can only get them from a friend who belongs to the studio. Plus, it keeps walk-ins from picking them up and using them.

When a friend or family member of a student redeems a "VIP" card, 2 things should happen:

- **The student IMMEDIATELY gets to pick a prize from a prize box.** If it's an adult who referred the new student, give them $5.00 credit for your Pro Shop.

- **The "VIP" card is put into a raffle bin.** Each card that is redeemed is good for one chance to win whatever prizes you are raffling off that month. We've raffled off game consoles, uniforms, and private lessons. Use your imagination, and make sure you are raffling off prizes that your students really want.

This program will work wonders for your referrals, if you do it right.

A FEW THINGS TO REMEMBER:

- **Don't run it all the time.** Do it three times a year – during "back-to-school", at the end of the school year, and in January. If you run it all the time it tends to be less effective.
- **Get good prizes**, and put them out for all to see!
- **Talk about it at the end of every class.** Also, hand out fliers and put up posters announcing the referral program.

All in all, it's pretty simple to do, and the rewards are worth the extra work. If you don't already have such a program in place, get this program going in your school immediately. Trust me, in a few months you'll be glad you did!

[7]

Principle #2

HOW TO INCREASE THE SIZE OF EVERY SALE IN YOUR MARTIAL ARTS SCHOOL

Remember when I asked you if you'd like to double the amount of money you initially receive from every student you enroll? Sounds good, right? But, I bet you're wondering just how you can accomplish this with every single sale. To be honest, it's not going to happen on every sale, but you can increase that initial payment drastically on most sales you make by using the following methods:

FIRST, RAISE YOUR RATES

You're probably charging way too little, anyway - likely much less than the market will accept. In fact, by being a "nice guy" and "not charging your students too much" you're taking food off your own table and putting it on theirs. I know that some of you may strongly disagree with this, but I ask you to withhold judgment until you read the following section where I will go into detail on how you should be setting your tuition rates.

Now, I don't suggest that you start charging your current students more; you'll lose too many of them that way. Instead, start charging the new rates for all the new members you enroll, and then work on upgrading your current members to unlimited or BBC memberships at a reduced rate that is comparable to the new higher tuition rates you've set. This way, you reward your current students for their loyalty, and you're still making more on every student.

Second, Upsell

The phrase, "Do you want to upsize your order?" has become synonymous with this concept. Offer add-ons when students enroll, such as one-time offers on equipment packages, extra training opportunities, private lesson packages, and so on. We'll discuss this more shortly.

Third, Sell in Bulk

Offer a greater overall discount for paying in advance when the student enrolls on a longer length of membership. Only a percentage of your new students will take you up on your offer, but those who do will represent a significant amount of income you would have missed had you not offered such an option.

And, so long as you implement all the things I advised you to do in the previous section on retention, there's absolutely nothing wrong with giving students a discount for paying their tuition up front. In fact, I offer a flat 10% discount for students who pay their entire tuition up front.

Typically, I find that it's only the people who are really committed to sticking around who take advantage of this discount. Just make sure you have a sign posted in your studio that clearly states, "No Refunds". Otherwise, you might eventually have a situation where someone pays up front, and later tries to get a partial refund of their payment after getting a case of lazy.

So, now that you have an idea of how we're going to increase the size of the sale, let's tackle the first item on the menu; namely, raising your tuition rates.

HOW TO SET YOUR MARTIAL ARTS TUITION RATES

One of the most common questions I receive from instructors, and the one that seems to cause most new instructors to have sleepless nights is, *"How much should I charge?"* This seemingly harmless question somehow ends up becoming an area of confusion and frustration for new instructors and seasoned studio owners alike. Mostly, the reasons for this boil down to the following:

- Many instructors place too little value on what they have to offer -
- And even those instructors who feel they are charging too little are often afraid to charge more, due to the possibility of losing current and future students to their competition -

First, I'll deal with both of these issues in turn. Then I'm going to provide you with multiple approaches that you can use to determine your tuition rates. Finally, I'll talk about other tuition considerations, such as how to offer scholarships and discounts.

REALITY DICTATES THAT YOU SHOULD VALUE WHAT YOU OFFER

I am going to be honest with you and tell you that I used to feel like instructors shouldn't charge "too much" for lessons. The thing is, that was back when I was operating from a limited perspective on how much it costs to run a full-time studio.

I changed my tune within the first few months of running a full-time location. After having to pay my rent, utilities, and insurance for a few months, I soon became a realist about how much I needed to charge to pay my bills and still make a decent income that I could comfortably live on.

I raised my rates soon after, and I've *never* regretted it.

Now, I realize that some of you may not have high overhead costs, and that's great. My bills weren't that high either, since I had started with almost nothing and had to start my studio on a shoestring budget. But even if you have zero overhead costs, there are other, very good reasons for charging adequately for your services.

WHY RAISING YOUR RATES WILL ATTRACT MORE STUDENTS

One reason is something that psychologists call social influence. Psychology professor Dr. Robert Cialdini of Arizona State University has done a great deal of research into what influences people to make certain buying decisions. One of the more interesting things he has discovered is that people have a tendency to believe that "expensive = good."

Cialdini relates the story of Chivas Regal scotch whiskey as an illustration of this principle. At first, the manufacturers of Chivas were having a hard time selling their product, so they decided to price their product much higher than the competition. The brand became a great success shortly thereafter and sales went through the roof.

How do you explain this? Simple. Value is based on perception. Chivas already had a quality product, but by pricing it lower consumers subconsciously perceived it to be of lesser value. By raising their prices they eliminated that perception and also gave the message to consumers that they did indeed make a quality product.

So, when you price your services at the bottom of the market, you are giving consumers the impression that your services are lower in quality. And, whether you believe it or not the fact is you are driving potential students away by under-pricing your services. Now, let's discuss different pricing strategies and how we can apply them to setting our tuition rates.

Pricing Strategy #1: the Law of Supply and Demand

Anyone who has taken Economics 101 knows the law of supply and demand, which tells us that scarcity creates demand, and demand drives prices up. You should be aware that when a service is not a commodity (easily copied and mass-produced), it is naturally in higher demand and worth more. Our services are unique because very few people make it to black belt and even fewer decide to teach. So when your services are in demand, you needn't be afraid to charge more.

If you are the only martial arts school in your area, charge appropriately according to what the market will bear. But how do you determine this? First, you should look at the cost of other comparable services, like golf and flight lessons for adults, and gymnastics and ballet lessons for children. Be sure to compare apples to apples when making this comparison! Break the cost down to hourly rates, and take into account whether the classes offer group or private instruction.

Second, you'll want to determine the income level of your area. At the time of this writing I believe that $100 per month is the absolute lowest tuition you should charge for two group classes per week. However, if you are located in an area where the average household income is higher than the national average ($51,914 in 2010) you should raise your rates accordingly.

Visit http://factfinder.census.gov to get economic statistics for your area.

Pricing Strategy #2: Using a Premium Pricing Strategy

So, what if you're in an area where there are a ton of martial arts studios? Should you get into a price war with your competition? Not on your life – or the life of your studio, for that matter! Competing on price is a foolish way to do business. For one, go back to Dr. Cialdini's research. If "expensive = good", then "cheap = bad" in the eyes of the consumer.

For an example of this, just look at Hyundai. When they first entered the market, they competed solely on price, offering cheap but mostly low-quality cars. But for years now, they've been improving their quality and offering one of the best warranties in the business.

Yet, many consumers still perceive Hyundai to be a cheap and unreliable product. Don't end up being the "Hyundai" of martial arts schools in your area. Instead, price your rates a minimum of 10% higher than your competitors, and make certain that you can justify this by offering a good quality service.

Pricing Strategy #3: Reverse Engineering

Figure out how much money you want to take home each month, minimum in order to live comfortably. Be reasonable – if you decide $60,000 a year take home is your goal, you need to make a profit of around $72,000 a year, or $6,000 a month. If your monthly overhead costs are $4,000 per month total, and you charge $100 per month tuition, then you'll hit your mark at 100 students. (I'd try to maintain between 105 and 110, just to account for seasonal fluctuations and attrition.)

By the way, just by increasing your tuition 30% and keeping your overhead costs constant at $4,000 per month, you'd increase your profits by nearly 45% to $9,000 per month or $108,000 per year. (Note: That's why I harp on keeping overhead costs down, and maximizing your profit margins. There's just no reason why you should be paying for more than 1,500 square feet of space or more than 1 or 2 part-time employees with only 110 students. See *Small Dojo Big Profits* and read *Developing Staff and Leadership Teams* for more on this topic.)

HOW TO COLLECT MORE TUITION PER STUDENT

Even if you don't want to raise your base tuition across the board by 30%, there are plenty of other ways to earn more tuition per student. For instance, you can host an added-profit event each month (like a special training seminar) that costs around $30 per student. Only a percentage will attend, but even if only 30% of 110 students attend you'll make an additional $1,000 for a few hours work. I'll talk about this in great detail in the next section, but I think you can see how this can significantly increase your school's income.

Also, as I mentioned in the previous section you can charge more for premium membership levels. I know a lot of people don't like the "black belt club" and "master's club" concepts, but no one says you have to call it that. How about having a "Gold level" and a "Platinum level" membership, and holding a few extra classes a week just for those students? You can charge 25% to 50% more per month for this added service. Or, you could have a basic membership that gets you two classes per week, and charge 10% more per month for each additional class per week that your students want to attend.

To wrap things up, pricing your tuition is really not all that difficult a task. The main thing you should remember is that your time and expertise are worth a lot more to your students than you may think. Price your services accordingly, and you will increase your profit and improve the financial stability of your studio.

THE FLIPSIDE: DISCOUNTS AND SCHOLARSHIPS

Yes, you have to make a profit when you're in business, but it's not all about the profit. I strongly believe that offering discounts and scholarships in your school is a great way to "pay it forward". I also believe that community service is something every martial arts school should do, but that's a topic for another book. For now, let's stick to the topic at hand, which is offering scholarships and discounts in your school.

OFFERING SCHOLARSHIPS

If you're like me, you started teaching in order to help people, not to become the Donald Trump or Bill Gates of the martial arts industry. Because of this, even after I got some common sense on the realities of what I needed to charge to feed my family and keep my school open, I still wanted to be able to reach under-privileged kids and lower-income adults with my services. There's an easy way to do this, and it's to offer a "scholarship" program in your studio. Basically, you set some criteria for what you will charge students based on income. You might choose to have a sliding scale, or to just offer reduced rates for people in financial need.

The important thing to remember is that you still aren't giving your services away for free. You still have to charge something to your scholarship students; otherwise they won't appreciate or value what you are doing. It also allows them to feel that they are contributing to your studio. Also, you have to make the student earn the scholarship. That means good or improving grades in school for kids, and work/study for adults. This will weed out the people who are just trying to get over on you, and it just makes good sense.

FAMILY DISCOUNTS

The most common type of discount program is a family discount. Be aware that most moms and dads want to have their children in the same activities (cuts down on confusion and drive time). Additionally, once one family member starts training others will often wish to follow suit.

However, for some families having three or more family members in martial arts can be prohibitively expensive. That's why you should offer a family discount program to make your programs more attractive and to encourage other family members to enroll.

A simple method to do this is to offer "x" percent discount for each additional family member. For example, our family program was 20% for the second family member, 30% for the third, 40% for the fourth, and so on. Just be reasonable when setting your family rates and remember that any money is better than none at all.

DISCOUNTS FOR SPECIAL GROUPS

In order to attract segments of the market that you may not normally attract, you may want to implement discount for certain groups. For example, if you live in a college town, you'll want to offer a student discount of between 10 and 25 percent of your regular rates. College students love this type of discount, and they'll tell their friends.

Also, an "over-55" discount is always a good idea. You'd be surprised how many retirees are interested in learning martial arts. Most of them have plenty of time on their hands, and some disposable income set aside for recreational activities. Be aware that for the most part retirees live on a fixed income, so discount programs are generally well received by this market segment.

Some schools offer discounts for military, police, EMS, and firefighters as well. Many of these people are influencers in their respective communities, and they are also part of a tight-knit professional community as well. Having them in your school can go a long way toward expanding your realm of influence, and it also serves as a subtle form of third-party endorsement for your school. Consider offering such a discount to attract these folks into your studio. Besides, they work hard and often do so for low pay; giving them a break is also a way of paying it forward in your school.

Corporate Discounts

Corporate discounts are another great way to attract students. Just look around for the major employers in your area, and contact their human resources department with an offer for a corporate discount on your services. More often than not, such employers will offer to list you in a benefits directory for their employees. This alone can bring in a significant amount of students each year, and may even lead to your teaching an "on-site" program.

A Final Action Item List for Setting Your Tuition Rates

Gather Your Data

✓ Call from a private phone line and get prices for all competing martial arts schools in your area. Be sure to ask about all additional costs, such as down payments, registration fees, and testing fees.

✓ Call all dance, gymnastics, cheer, and music schools in your area, and get their tuition rates as well. If you offer after-school pick-up, call the day-cares and other competing programs as well.

✓ Call the YMCA programs, rec centers, and any other part-time martial arts programs, and find out what they charge.

Evaluate Your Data

✓ Now, create a chart using Excel or a spreadsheet in Word. List every business, and how much their tuition *and fees* are for each one. Be sure to calculate in the hidden costs that many schools don't reveal up front; you're going to have to dig for this when you do your market research.

✓ Add up all the fees to average the total monthly cost for each school or business. Remember, we want the actual cost.

✓ Determine the highest cost, the lowest, cost, and the average cost.

Set Your Rates

✓ If you're a new school, start off at ten percent lower than your nearest competitor until you enroll enough students to pay your overhead plus 20% each month.

✓ If you're an established school, you should be charging 10% more than your highest-priced competitor. This is because you want to establish yourself as the price leader in your market, and also to position your school as the "best" martial art school in your area. If this makes zero sense to you, go back and read this chapter again.

Most school owners find after following this process that they are charging much less than their strongest competitors. Do it and you may be surprised at what you find out regarding what people in your area are willing to pay for activities such as martial arts lessons. Then, set your tuition rates accordingly. And, you can do so while resting soundly in the knowledge that by implementing all the retention strategies in this book, you are offering a customer service experience that is of a much higher quality than your competitors.

[8]

Upselling and Overcoming Price Issues

THE ART OF THE UPSELL

Having an "upsell" in your martial arts studio is a great way to increase the size of every sale you make. Fast food restaurants discovered this and McDonald's did it so well that all the other fast food joints copied their approach. You'll be hard-pressed to walk into a fast food restaurant these days without the person at the counter asking if you "want fries with that", or if you'd like to "up-size" your meal (and your waistband, as well).

And, it's now common for other businesses to use the upsell to increase their profits. For example, recall the last time you made a significant purchase of electronics or appliances; I can almost bet that you were offered a "protection plan" for the item you purchased. Car dealers are also experts at using the upsell. They advertise the bare bones car price, but then they take you for a test drive in the luxury version of the car you're considering for purchase. Once you've seen the version with all the bells and whistles, it's a sure bet that you'll want at least some of those upgrades in your new vehicle.

So how can we also use this profit-increasing tactic, and in such a way that we remain aligned with our ethics and morals as well? Quite simply, by adding value to the customer's purchase, and doing so in such a way that they feel quite comfortable with paying more at the time of the sale. Here are three ways you can do this.

MEMBERSHIP UPSELLS

The easiest upsell you'll ever use is the membership upsell. Granted, you'll have an upsell for the client down the road when they qualify for your Black Belt Club. However, there's nothing that says you can't start offering an upgraded membership from the day they walk in your door.

My favorite membership upsell is the simplest one to do, and that's to offer a "basic", a "mid-grade", and a "premium" membership. This is the same tactic that gas stations use to charge you more for your fuel; the regular unleaded gas works just the same as the "premium" gas to get you from point A to point B, but oil companies know that car aficionados want to baby their vehicles. So, they add a few chemicals to your basic gasoline and voila! We pay more at the pump (well, I don't... but you might).

Likewise, you are always going to have some customers who want just the barebones basic membership, and you're always going to have other people who will want the very best. Some of this is psychological, and some of it is sociological; regardless of the reasons why, it behooves you to have a variety of service and membership offerings in place.

I find that the sweet spot is having three membership options to select from. So, how do you justify charging more for a membership? That's simple, by offering more. My basic membership is for two classes a week, the "mid-grade" membership is for three classes a week, and the "premium" membership is for unlimited classes.

I increase the base tuition rate by 25% for the mid-grade and by 50% for the premium membership. The fact is, a percentage of people want to train more, and some want to train less. So, I allow them to do so and I charge them for the extra training. And, this is perfectly ethical and justifiable, considering that every martial art school owner faces the same dilemma; that being the limits of time and space in delivering instruction. People understand this, *and they expect to pay more for getting more;* it's just common sense.

PRIVATE LESSON ADD-ONS

Again, some people who join your studio are going to want to go all the way with their training. They are going to want to attend every class they can, and get all the help they can to make their learning experience better. These are the best candidates for selling private lesson package upgrades on enrollment.

There are a few ways to package private lessons for new students. You can increase the monthly tuition payment and offer a weekly or a monthly private lesson as part of the package. So, the student pays $300 a month, they get a weekly private lesson, and they get to attend unlimited classes. You'd be amazed how many people will be willing to take you up on this.

Or, you can offer a block of private lessons at a one-time discount that is only for new members. Maybe your private lessons normally cost $70 each, so you could offer a block of 10 lessons for $499 on a one-time discount only, or 4 lessons for $249 again for a one-time discount only. Many new students will take you up on this offer when they join, especially if you let them know they can use them at any time, and explain that this can come in handy later on down the road if they need extra help at some point in their training.

Finally, you can sell a private-lesson-only membership. This is for people who just want to do private lessons. No matter what area you are in, there are going to be people who can afford and who will pay you to just get private instruction. These people don't want to be in a class sharing your attention with others. They want one-on-one instruction, and they will be willing to pay you handsomely for your undivided attention.

For these folks, you should enroll them on a membership just like any other client, but for private lessons only. And, you should offer a discount of some sort so they have a reason to do this. Even though wealthy people may have money to spend, they are still careful with their money and like a good deal. (Note: That's how often they became wealthy in the first place; lottery winners and NFL rookies usually end up becoming broke because they don't know how to manage their money. I've seen the same thing happen with school owners who experience sudden growth in their schools; they pitter away their money and then end up broke. Don't make that mistake.)

So, offer them three different packages; one for one private lesson a week, one for two private lessons a week, and one for three private lessons a week. Let's say I normally charged $100 an hour for private lessons; here's how I would price these private-lesson-only memberships:

- One a week - $90 a session, or $360 a month
- Two a week - $80 a session, or $640 a month
- Three a week - $70 a session, or $840 a month

I would also make them enroll for a minimum of three months at a time, and I would offer them a discount of 10% off for paying for all three months at once. I've used a lot of different methods for charging for private lessons in the past, and this method is the best I've seen for maximizing the amount you are paid up front, as well as for keeping high-paying private lesson clients around longer.

I think you can also see the financial leverage inherent to selling large packages of private lessons. If you just sell one three-month package at the 3x a week rate each month, that's an additional $27,000 a year in income... and that's only if your clients just stick around for three months. If you manage to keep some of them around longer, the math gets even better. This can be a game-changer for many school owners, as just one client a month can pay the overhead costs on a typical *Small Dojo Big Profits* studio operation. And if you ever wondered how personal fitness trainers make $100,000.00 a year, that's how the smart ones do it.

ONE-TIME EQUIPMENT PACKAGE DISCOUNT OFFERS

Another easy way to increase the amount you make up front off every single student you enroll is to offer them a one-time discount on a package deal for equipment they will need in order to train. This package should include items that they will need to purchase in the first six months of their training, and you should offer them a nice discount to encourage them to buy when they enroll. Make it clear that if they buy the equipment piecemeal later on, or if they decide to buy the package later, it will cost them more.

Examples of equipment you can include in such a package:

- Uniform or upgraded uniform
- Patches
- Sparring gear
- Striking and kicking pads (for practicing at home with mom and dad)
- Practice weapons (if you offer such training)
- Gear bag to put it all in (helps if it has your school logo on it)

In order to make this profitable, you must have a wholesale account with an equipment supplier who offers a decent wholesale discount. Your profit margin has to be at least 50% so you double your money on everything you sell at retail. This will allow you the wiggle room to offer a deeper discount on the package when they enroll.

Here's an example of a one-time offer discount for a new student package:

New Student Discount On Equipment:

* *Uniform or upgraded uniform ($40 retail)*

* *Patches ($15 retail)*

* *Sparring gear ($100 retail)*

* *Striking and kicking pads ($50 retail)*

* *Foam chuks ($12 retail)*

* *Gear bag to put it all in ($30 retail)*

Regular retail cost *if purchased separately:* **$247.00**

Discounted price *if purchased in the "new student package" on the date of enrollment: Just **$197**! Please note, this is a one-time offer only good on the date of your enrollment, so be sure to take advantage of it today to save.*

That's a 20% discount, or a savings of $50.00. To help you sell these packages, make sure you have a laminated flier with the entire package listed item-by-item as I've itemized them above with prices, and include the discounted percentage and total savings at the bottom. Show the client the flier after they sign their membership agreement, but before you take their initial payment, so they have the option of adding it on.

So long as your profit margins on all this gear are at least 50%, you'll still be profiting $73.50 on each package using the prices above; this can easily mean an extra $750 to $1,000 a month in profit for your studio. Obviously, you need to play with the numbers based on what your suppliers actually charge you for the gear you decide to include in your new member package. I also suggest that you use whole numbers for the total undiscounted cost, and even/odd pricing (99's and 97's) for the discounted price in order to maximize the psychological impact of the discounted price.

You should also be selling that package in your Pro Shop at a 10% discount all year long, as it will help boost your Pro Shop sales as well (see the Profit Boosting Principle #3 coming up in the next section for more on this).

How to Make Price a Non-Issue

As you go about the task of increasing your rates, I can assure you that you will meet with resistance at some point if you're pricing your memberships at a premium price point. In my experience, however, you will meet with some price resistance at almost any price point; it's just typical buyer psychology. To make things easier on you when you are closing sales, here are couple of things I suggest you do to increase the amount of intro-to-membership conversions you are getting and to increase your bottom line without having to lower your rates.

Charge an Appropriate Rate for Intros

Some people will say pre-qualifying prospects is a waste of time, but I've always done it to weed out tire kickers and to increase my conversions. One way to accomplish this is to stop doing free trials, and instead replace them with a $19.95 or $29.95 one-week introductory program. Yes, you will get fewer leads, but you will get more qualified prospects since the tire kickers will be less likely to pay for an introductory program. Also, by pricing the trial at roughly 25% of your monthly rates, you are setting the expected price in the prospect's mind. This can help prevent sticker shock when they are ready to enroll.

Have a "Down-Sell"

If someone balks at your regular membership rates, offer a membership package with fewer features and benefits at a reduced rate. Since my basic membership includes two classes a week, if someone can't "afford" my regular membership I'll offer them a one-day per week membership at 70% of the regular tuition. 70% of something is better than 100% of nothing, right?

Emphasize the Value of the Total Package

Make sure you have all your features and benefits of your memberships written out in bullet points, and go through them line-by-line when you are enrolling new members. Also, be sure to place a value on the total package and tell the client how much they are saving by taking the package rate: "Remember, with the Gold Belt membership package you get two classes per week, a 10% discount on all school events, a 10% discount on Pro Shop purchases, 50% off testing fees, a uniform and patches worth $150.00, and unlimited access to the member's section of our website. This is a $1,400.00 value, but the package price is only $899.00."

Make it Easy to Pay

Offer several payment options and methods. Make sure you can accept all forms of payment. And again, offer at least three different payment plans to allow your students to "budget" their payments.

Overcoming Objections: How to Ferret Out the Real Issue

Oftentimes, the real issue that is causing someone to hesitate before enrolling in your school isn't price. So, it's important that you know how to ferret out the real reason they aren't comfortable with enrolling. Knowing how to do this will easily increase your conversions by 10 to 20%.

Here's the easiest way to go about it. When the prospect says "I'll have to think about it" or "I need to discuss this with my spouse", simply say:

- *"Mrs. Jones, you told me that Johnny had a great time in our classes, so it must be something else that is giving you pause."*
- *"Is it me? Did I say or do something to offend you?" <Pause, listen>*
- *"Is it the class times?" <Pause, listen>*
- *"Is it the length of the membership?" <Pause, listen>*
- *"Then, is it the cost?" <Pause, listen>*

Once you ferret out the real reason why they aren't quite ready to enroll, then you can deal with that issue and ease the customer's concerns. Chances are really good that it's not something you said or did; more likely, it'll be one of the other issues.

If it's your class times, point out that they can come to either an earlier or a later class if their schedule changes. Usually, moms and dads have concerns about soccer or some other sport season that's coming up. Make sure they know you'll be flexible with them when that time comes, and point out the flexibility in your schedule as well.

If it's membership length, offer them the right to cancel within the first 30 days for any reason. Then let them know that they can cancel due to an extended illness or injury, or if they move more than 25 miles from your school (you should have these clauses in your membership agreements). Just be sure they understand that on the 31st day, you expect them to be fully committed to taking martial arts for the remainder of their membership.

And, if it's cost? Well, we dealt with that in the previous section. Go back over their options for membership, and be sure to restate everything they're getting with their membership. Hopefully, you can either come to a membership level and payment schedule that fits their budget, or they'll realize that it's worth the cost.

[9]

Profit-Boosting Principle #3

Increasing the Frequency of the Sale

By increasing the frequency of the sale, you can actually make more net profit in your martial art school without increasing your overhead, and without increasing your enrollment, either. However, this is a concept that confuses many martial art school owners, because of the fact that our industry is based around selling memberships on monthly installment payments. That's why most school owners look at me like I'm crazy when I tell them they need to increase the frequency at which their clients give them money.

Getting people to pay you more often can seem like an impossibility when you are charging for martial arts lessons on a monthly basis, which is why you need to look at other ways to bring in money to your school. Once you start looking at other products and services that you can offer to your clients in addition to their membership it's easy to find opportunities to increase the frequency of the sale.

The way to do this is by implementing what I call *added-profit centers* in your school. A "profit center" is any division of a business that adds more revenue. For our purposes, an "added profit center" refers to ways you can increase your profits that are *added* to what you make from your primary revenue stream, which is charging money for martial arts instruction.

I call this money "gravy money", because you get it on top of your "meat", which is teaching martial arts lessons. Of course, this results in your school having *multiple profit centers* instead of just one, thus multiplying the frequency of the sale. There are three primary added profit centers you can implement in a martial arts school, and here they are in no particular order:

SELLING EQUIPMENT AND APPAREL

Monthly Pro Shop specials and seasonal Pro Shop sales encourage your students to spend more money in your school. Try to think of things your students will buy anyway, and offer them a way to do just that at your school. Replacement and back-up uniforms, summer uniforms, t-shirts, caps, jewelry... these are all things your students spend money on anyway. I'll explain more about how to do this shortly.

SPECIAL EVENTS

Special events are great added profit centers. I suggest you alternate who you're selling them to by offering a free event one month for each age classification (kids, teens, adults) and a paid event the next month. Free events can include parties for kids and social gatherings for adults that are designed to bring in new members (buddy nights, Halloween parties, and so on). Paid events include "parent's night out" events for kids, in-house tournaments, hosting birthday parties, and hosting special topic seminars for adults.

On the following pages, I'll provide you with several ideas for paid special events that you can host in your school. However, it's up to you to promote them and run them in such a way that your students feel that they got their money's worth. For kids, this means making sure they have a ton of fun at every event. For adults, it means making sure they have fun, and that they learn something at every event. Keep that in mind as you're planning these events throughout the year.

Testing Fees

Charging testing fees definitely should not make up a major source of your income. However, if you spend a considerable amount of your time outside of normal class hours conducting exams and promotions ("graduations"), by all means you should charge something for it. I don't think this needs a lot of explanation; however, at the end of this section I will go into detail about how to run a graduation event so you understand the importance of using these events for retention, and not just as a justification for charging testing fees.

How to Sell More from Your Pro Shop

Increasing your Pro Shop equipment sales is simply a matter of having a method of operations that you follow each month to increase your sales. There are a number of steps you can take to do this. I'll list each one and explain what it involves so you can understand just how simple it is to increase your Pro Shop sales.

Use Clear and Visible Pricing

If people can't see a price, often they are too embarrassed to ask about an item for fear they won't be able to afford it. So, get a pricing gun or some write-on price tags and use them on all your items.

Display Items Openly

People shop with all five senses. Shoppers want to touch what they are going to buy. For apparel, people need to be able to hold an item up to their bodies (at the very least) to see how it will fit. Display your merchandise openly and where it is easy for shoppers to touch and feel.

ROTATE YOUR STOCK

If shoppers see the same thing every day, week after week, month after month... they start to ignore it. Shake up your displays by changing them regularly. This also will help you keep them clean and dust-free.

OFFER PACKAGE DEALS

Remember the package deal we put together for new students earlier in the book? Have these packages ready to go in your Pro Shop display, or use a wire wall rack to display the package all the time with clear pricing and the discount marked on a nice display (I like using neon foam board cut in a starburst pattern). Move it around every so often when you rotate your merchandise.

USE SPECIAL EVENT TIE-INS

As you'll see later in this book, special events can be a great source of Pro Shop sales. While I like to bundle an item (like Glow Chuks, etc.) in with the cost of admission to a special event, you can also sell those items in your Pro Shop prior to the event so students have them beforehand (also a great way to boost attendance). In addition, some students will want to buy upgraded versions of weapons and gear they've used in your seminars. Keep such items on hand and in stock around the time you plan to use them in seminars in order to boost sales.

HAVE A FEATURED SALE ITEM OF THE MONTH

You can tie this in with a seminar, or with a movie or other popular martial arts event. Or, just pick something that you think will move fast when you put it out for sale. I know some schools will create a fresh t-shirt design every other month to sell in their Pro Shop. Many students will buy every single t-shirt design you offer, so long as they are stylish and comfortable. Be sure to use good quality t-shirts in contemporary styles if you decide to do this.

USE BBC TIE-INS

Remember my "weapon of the month" BBC curriculum? Students love it and it sells a lot of practice weapons. I'm sure you can think of other ways to tie-in BBC classes with Pro Shop sales.

HOLD A HOLIDAY SALE

Every year my holiday sales produce a few extra grand of profit that I wouldn't have otherwise. This really helps make up for those last two weeks of December when enrollments are low. I'll discuss how to plan and execute one properly later in this book.

GET RID OF STALE MERCHANDIZE QUARTERLY

Anything that doesn't sell for six months or more needs to be discounted and sold quarterly. I suggest a 25% discount for quarterly inventory reduction and a 50% discount for end of year inventory reduction sales.

SELL USED EQUIPMENT AT A DISCOUNT TO FINANCE REPLACEMENTS

Whenever I need to replace equipment, I remove worn gear from use when it starts to get unsightly, but before it becomes unserviceable. Then, I mark it as "used" and sell it at 50% off retail in the Pro Shop. This is how I finance getting new equipment. Students like getting a good deal and I like that I don't have to pay more out of pocket for new replacement gear... a win-win.

My Quick and Easy Guide to Profiting From Birthday Parties

If you're like most martial arts business owners you're always looking for simple ways to make some extra money and recruit new students. One of the easiest methods to recruit kids to your program while bringing in extra income is through hosting birthday parties.

Now, before you begin to pass judgment, hear me out. I know of gymnastics centers that do a significant amount of their business on birthday parties alone. And, believe it or not, if you teach kids it's the dance and gymnastics centers that are your main competition, not the YMCA karate program down the street.

Although it may not be in the scope of duties that you envisioned yourself performing when you opened your studio, if you teach kids and are not yet hosting birthday parties you are overlooking a major source or referrals and income for your martial arts business. Done properly, they will increase your exposure and bring in additional income with a very small investment of time and money.

How to Run a Birthday Party Event That Is Headache-Free in 7 Easy Steps

1. **Set up some games or activities beforehand so when the kids start coming in they have something to do.** Have them remove their shoes and let them come out on the floor. A good choice is to have an assistant holding a soft pad, play some upbeat music and start a line with the kids coming up and kicking the pad. Note: Just demonstrate the kick once or twice, then encourage them and give them praise no matter how well they do – if you try to teach your whole style to them or over-correct them today you'll spoil the mood.

2. **Once all the kids are there, show them how to line up, with the birthday boy or girl taking the first spot in line** (this is important – the birthday party host always gets to be the center of attention all day long!)

3. **Briefly explain your "school rules" in a way that is non-intimidating.** Tell the kids that in order to have lots of fun today, everyone has to follow the rules. Kids are used to this and will generally behave once they are given boundaries for their behavior. Emphasize good sportsmanship!

4. **Have a fun 20-minute martial arts class for them.** Play some age-appropriate games interspersed with some basic martial arts training – but nothing that involves children working with each other – only solo practice! This is to avoid the possibility that you will have a high-strung kid with poor impulse control who will get into trouble by being too rough. Save yourself some headaches and stick to simple things that don't require a partner.

5. **Play some games.** Some suggested games are "Sensei Says", dodge ball (use those "Splash Balls" that you can purchase at Wal-Mart in the pool toys section – they are soft, durable, and heavy enough to throw well at distances of 15-20 feet), and relay races. Have some inexpensive prizes ready to be handed out, like martial arts stickers, martial arts dog tags, and foam rubber ninja stars. Give everyone an opportunity to win something, so everyone has a good time.

6. **After they are good and tired, it's cake and presents time!** Bow them out and send them to the parents for snacks, cake and opening presents.

7. **Prepare "Thank you!" cards beforehand with "Free Karate" guest passes in them, addressed from the host.** Before everyone leaves, give them to the host to hand out to his or

her guests. Announce out loud that "Johnny has something to give to everyone for coming today – be sure to see him before you leave!" Don't miss this opportunity to recruit new students for your martial arts business!

You might also want to get names and phone numbers of guests from the host parent so you can follow up on the guest pass they received the following week. Once again, this is another opportunity to recruit new members for your martial arts business.

Important points:

• Set up a table for eating in the viewing/reception area, well away from the training area. Make it clear that no one is to eat or drink in the training area!

• Communicate your plan to the parent of the birthday boy or girl beforehand. Make it clear that you have a specific way to conduct the party, but that after your part is done they can do whatever they wish (as long as it does not violate school policy).

• As a martial arts business owner, your time is money. Make it clear to the parents that they are paying for your time. Keep track of the time and charge them accordingly for each half-hour they are present in your studio (I suggest at least $99 or more for a 45-minute party plus $50 for every additional half-hour you are present). Otherwise, you will have kids at your school all afternoon. Trust me, this is important.

• Finally, designate the times and dates you are available and stick to them. Set dates well in advance and require a 50% non-refundable deposit for all parties. This will save you the headache of having last-minute cancellations because a parent was using you as a back-up in case they couldn't get a reservation at Chuck-E-Cheese.

Hopefully this has given you some ideas on how to host profitable birthday party events in your martial arts school. Remember, the key to profiting with these is to advertise them constantly, to organize each one using the system I outline above, and to charge enough to make it worth your time to do them.

An Added Profit Special Event for Every Month of the Year

The following is a list of special events that you can hold throughout the year. Holding one of these events each month will help you to boost your profits and also help you keep your students happy all year long. And, I'd like to emphasize the "keeping your students happy" part, because there's more to these events than a simple profit motive.

While you may think that these events are all just ways to make more money from your existing clientele, in fact they are a great way to keep the excitement level high in your school. In addition, they are a great opportunity to bond with your students as well. And, I don't have to tell you at this point how important those two side benefits will be to increasing your retention, which you should know by now is a major component of Profit-Boosting Principle #1.

And a note to my international readers... just because the majority of these events revolve around American holidays, it doesn't mean you can't use them. I'm sure with just a little work you can adapt these same events for use in your own country and culture, perhaps in conjunction with holidays that are customary in your area.

Also, notice that I have a lot of the fun kids events scheduled during the school year in the Spring and Fall months. That's because you want your younger students to have a reason to tell their friends about your school. Give them an amazingly fun event to attend, and I guarantee you they are going to rave about it to their friends. Believe me, this will help your kids programs grow quickly.

JANUARY

Pro Shop Clearance Sale: January is the best time to have a Pro Shop clearance sale. For one, you're going to have a lot of inventory left over from the previous year that you'll want to clear out. Also, a lot of your clients will be cash-strapped from all those Christmas and holiday shopping bills coming due, so your Pro Shop sales will be low otherwise. For these reasons, use January to clear out all of your stale inventory from the previous year.

Anything that hasn't moved for six months or more is fair game. Set up a discount table and put all that old gear and apparel on it. Mark it all down at least 50% or more.

Why such a steep discount? Look, you aren't married to that stuff, and you have operating capital tied up in it. In retail, you need to keep turning over the money you have invested in inventory so you can make a profit. If you don't, your profits will fall and you'll be stuck with a Pro Shop full of stuff that no one wants. So, sell it off, get your money back, and reinvest that money into inventory that will sell.

New Year's Eve Sleepover: See the "June" event below.

FEBRUARY

Valentine's Day Parent's Night Out Event: Guess what? Every so often parents need some time by themselves, which is no surprise to those of you who have children. Well, it so happens that Valentine's Day is a time when almost every couple with kids is having a hard time finding a sitter. So, having a fun event where parents will know their kids are safe on Valentine's Day (or the Friday or Saturday before) is a great way to make extra money.

MARCH

Student Seminar for Adult Students: Pick a topic that your students don't normally get to cover in detail in class, or something that your students have been begging you to learn. I actually suggest that you hold one of these events every other month. See the section that follows for more on hosting satisfying and profitable adult seminars and events.

April

Glow Chuk Seminar: Glow Chuck Seminars are a great event to hold for your kids. Children love learning to swing a pair of nunchaku, and they love it even more when they glow in the dark. I suggest that you price this event by packaging the chuks in the cost of the event. Also, make it long enough so that parents have some time to go out and have dinner while their kids are having fun.

May

Summer School Tournament: I like to hold in-school tournaments twice a year, so holding one in October and one in April or May spreads them out nicely. A good in-school tournament is a killer profit-generator, and it's also a great event for increasing school esprit de corps as well. Emphasize good sportsmanship and celebrate camaraderie to ensure that everyone has a good time and that they all go home with a smile on their face.

June

Summer Sleep Over: It's nice to do a Parent's Night Out Event as a sleep over and lock-in, at least one night a year. Make sure you plan it all out, and have fun activities scheduled throughout the night until midnight (even if most of the kids will be sacked out by then). Pizza and drinks are a must. Make sure you have male and female chaperons or staff members present at all times, and make it clear that you welcome parent volunteers. (The best policy is to never be in a situation where you or a staff member or volunteer is alone in a room with a child – period.) The fee should be around $50 per child unless you're feeling exceptionally charitable.

JULY

Parent/Child Seminar: This is a special night where parents can come in and workout with their kids – having a "Kicking Pad and Focus Mitt Parent/Child Seminar" is a good way to do this. This is a class where you teach the parent how to coach their child at home using simple square hand targets and kicking paddles that you also offer for sale at the seminar, or that you offer as a package deal with the cost of participation. You can also halve the cost of participation if the parent redeems a VIP pass for a free month of classes, as a way to encourage parents to enroll in classes.

AUGUST

Ninja Nite: Kids love Ninja Nite! This is basically a Parent's Night Out event that is ninja themed. You'll plan and play games that are ninja-skills based. When I hold them, we teach a foam nunchuk form, have a contest to see who can move the most silently, we have a throwing star contest (with foam rubber stars using a refrigerator box with cut-outs for the target, or suction cup stars with targets drawn on the mirrors with dry erase markers). You can also tell ninja stories, and you can even let the kids come dressed up as ninjas. Kids will talk about this event all year long if done right, and it is a great money-maker as well. Send each kid home with a foam star and a pair of foam chuks and that's all they'll talk about for weeks.

SEPTEMBER

Laser Challenge Night: Go purchase five or more sets of laser tag guns and harnesses at your local Toys R' Us. Set up your school using Wavemasters, folding mats, and large boxes (go to appliance stores for these) as upright obstacles to hide behind. Split kids up in teams and let them play for fifteen minutes per group, rotating groups through all night long. Have some video game consoles and videos set up for the kids who are waiting to play, and have snacks as well. Again, run this event right and kids will be talking about it all year long.

October

Pumpkin Tournament: These are always a hit. Go out and buy some small, medium, large, and one huge pumpkin (grand prize) to use for division prizes and a bunch of medals too, and have an in-school tournament for your students. And as funny as it sounds, if you get large pumpkins your younger students will think getting a big pumpkin is a really cool prize.

November

Holiday Shopping Drop-Off Day: This event is designed to give parents a chance to go shopping without having to pawn their kids off on grandma, the neighbors, etc. This is basically a short half-day karate camp held on a Saturday. The best day to do this is really on Black Friday (the day after Thanksgiving), but you have to promote the heck out of it to make it happen. Otherwise, I suggest you do it on the weekend after Thanksgiving weekend.

Christmas and Holiday Secret Shopping Day: This is a day when parents and spouses can come in and buy (or order) presents for their kids and loved ones in secret. If you hold it on the weekend of or weekend after Thanksgiving and advertise and promote it heavily among your clientele, you'll have a great turnout.

DECEMBER

Holiday Karate Day Camp: This is a great way to increase your profits when the kids are out of school. Parents of school-age kids often are at a loss for what to do with their kids over the holiday break when they're at work. By hosting a holiday camp, you are also providing them with a much needed service for which they'll gladly pay. The key to filling it is to start advertising it the month prior (as it is with all special events). Be sure to price it less than what it costs to put a kid in a local daycare for the week.

HOW TO PLAN AND HOST PROFITABLE SPECIAL EVENTS FOR YOUR ADULT STUDENTS

When most martial arts school owners think of special events, they probably envision Ninja Nights, sleepovers, and other lock-in type events for children. Rarely, however, do such school owners consider hosting special events for their adult students.

The school owner may believe that their adult students are too busy or too broke to attend such an event, or that they have to bring in a "big-name" martial artist to teach in order to get anyone to come. And, we all know how much those "name" martial artists charge for their services (and rightly so; they have bills just like everyone else).

However, increasing your profits in your martial arts school with adult special events is a lot easier than you might think. There are a ton of special events you can teach yourself that will increase your bottom line at the end of the month. The key is choosing the right ones so that you get a healthy turnout and structuring them in such a way that they make a decent profit.

Here are some guidelines for running special events for your adult students in your martial arts classes:

- ✓ First, find out what your adult students want. This involves more than just taking an informal vote in your next adult class. Take the time to write out a short survey, and make sure all your adult students fill it out anonymously. Have a drop box that they can leave them in by the door as they exit the studio.

✓ In the survey, I suggest that you list several topics covering a wide variety of subject matter that your students can choose from. This can include sparring, an in-school tournament, competition preparation, forms, self-defense vs. weapons, a weapons class, a class covering testing requirements, weapons sparring, a fitness course, grappling, pressure points; the possibilities are endless.

✓ Be sure to include a write-in blank as well, so students can write in suggestions that you haven't thought of.

✓ Also, ask them what times and dates they are available to attend and that are most convenient for them. You may also inquire as to the length of time that they would be willing to train during such an event.

✓ Finally, ask them what they might be willing to pay for a one-hour, a 3-4 hour, and an all-day seminar or event. Be sure to give them several options that they can choose from in various price ranges. Their responses may surprise you!

Once you have collected that information, read the responses carefully and tally up your results. Make note of special suggestions, especially for events you didn't initially consider. You may find some really good ideas here.

After you have the suggestions tallied up, pick the events, dates, and times that proved to be most popular, and start planning your event. Don't get miffed if some of the answers are a little curt or if your students want to learn things from outside your system. Instead, you should thank your lucky stars that you are finding out what your clients really want before your students drop out of your classes.

You can always go get trained and certified in areas that you have little or no experience in, if that's what your students are looking for. There are tons of classes for instructors who desire to organize programs in grappling, fitness and weight loss, weapons, and so forth. It's never too late to put your student cap back on and go learn the information so you can share it with your students.

[10]

Other Ways to Increase the Frequency of Purchase

PREPPING FOR SUMMER AND THE HOLIDAYS

When summer and the Christmas holidays roll around, some school owners rejoice while other wait in grim preparation for what is often their worst months of the year. Yes, revenues and enrollments can dip during the holiday and summer months, despite how the sunny folks in the industry magazines attempt to convince you otherwise. Regardless of the circumstances, in order to keep your overall profits high you need to know how to keep your revenue up and constant all year long.

This means making up for lost revenue caused by decreased enrollments during times of the year when you know enrollments will drop off temporarily. And how can you do this? For the most part, it boils down to planning ahead and adapting to the circumstances. This involves nothing more than making sure you have some extra income generators running over the summer and holiday months, and also having some killer specials going to attract new students all year long.

Summer and Holiday Income Generators

Martial Arts Day Camps

By far, the best summer and holiday income generators are karate day camps. That's the good news.

The bad news? They are a ton of work! Even so, without them you may find yourself in dire straits over the holidays and during those slower summer months. That's why I suggest school owners knuckle under and learn to enjoy running holiday and summer day camps each year.

The key to running successful martial arts day camps is having a proven plan to follow. Planning and organization are the keys to success in running camps. Good planning and organization will make the difference between making tons of extra cash over the summer or working your fingers to the bone for little extra gain.

If you have no idea how to run a camp, I suggest you get my summer karate camp system (AfterSchoolKarateProgram.com) and read it through. Then, follow that simple system to success this summer and over the holidays. You'll potentially add several thousand dollars to your bottom line each month to boot.

Holiday Sales

Holiday sales are a great way to boost your profits during those slow holiday weeks between mid-November and January 2nd. The key is to get your holiday catalogs out as early as possible and to set a date for your holiday sale by the first of November. I suggest you hold your sale the weekend after Thanksgiving.

Also, set your deadline for getting Christmas orders in at a date that's early enough to ensure that all your orders arrive a week before Christmas. That's to give parents enough time to pick them up. Talk to your supplier and ask when the last date is that they can guarantee delivery before you close for the Christmas holiday.

SUMMER SPECIALS

Many parents are of the mindset that they can just enroll their kids in a "summer activity" to keep them occupied for a few months. This attitude is common among parents, so why fight it? The market dictates what the market wants, so instead of trying to fight it, simply give them what they want each summer!

Every summer I offer a six-week summer karate special that includes a free uniform, a private lesson, and six weeks of group classes for a fantastic price. I know that parents are hard-wired to enroll their kids in short-term programs over the summer, so I just look at it as a long-term intro program and don't worry about the fact that half those kids won't stay past summer.

The upside though is that half of them WILL stay past summer – which will not only boost my short-term income during the summer months... it boosts my long-term income as well.

How to Sell Martial Arts Lessons During the Holidays

Let's talk about selling martial arts lessons over the holidays. As you're already aware, most consumers are focused more on buying things for the holidays during this time of year; presents, decorations, food for the family gatherings, gas or plane tickets for family trips, and so forth. So, in order to sell your programs over the holidays, you have to be thinking in "holiday mode".

The idea is to become a part of that holiday spending spree by making your programs something the consumer would want to purchase as part of their normal holiday spending. In addition, you need to ease the sting of buying a bit for those folks who have most of their disposable income allotted to the above-mentioned holiday expenditures.

How do you do this? In two ways:

1. By selling holiday gift certificates and packages -
2. And, by allowing people the option of deferring their payments until the following year -

Allow me to explain each approach, because they require different tactics to close the sale.

Selling Gift Certificates and Gift Packages

First, gift certificates and gift packages – you should have gift certificates and gift packages in several different price points:

- One at around $50 ($49) – This should include either a month of classes or two weeks with a free uniform
- One at around $100 ($99) – This should include a month of classes and a nicer uniform, or an additional piece of equipment
- And, one at around $150 to $200 ($149 or $199) – This should include a month of classes, plus everything a new student needs to begin training – uniform, sparring gear, a striking pad, and a bag to hold it all in

Now, rather than having to print up special gift certificates in several denominations, just go to Office Depot or a similar store with a print shop and order custom gift certificate. That way, you have a record of what you sold, and to whom, and for how much.

Be sure to have enough of the items in your packages on hand to sell. People will want to gift wrap something and put it under the tree, so have them in stock when they come in to buy. And although it's not necessary, it's also a nice touch to have holiday gift bags to put the customer's items in when they check out.

DEFERRED PAYMENT MEMBERSHIP SALES

How many times have you had someone call or come in for an intro course in November or December, only to tell you, "We'll be back after the holidays." Bull. They may intend to come back, but chances are very good they won't. So, you have to hook them right then and there or you'll likely lose them forever.

So, I tell them, "I know it's the holidays and that money can be tight this time of year. How about we just set your first payment for sometime in January or February of next year?" Realize that they are still going to pay the same amount of tuition. Either you roll their balance into next year's membership when it comes time to renew, or you divide and spread out the month or two they "skip" into their monthly payments over the course of the rest of the year.

Either way, you still make the same amount of money, and you enroll a student you would have lost otherwise. And, although it won't really help your numbers in December, in January and February it will really boost your bottom line when those payments begin.

HOW TO RUN AN EXCITING GRADUATION CEREMONY THAT BOTH ATTRACTS AND KEEPS STUDENTS

"Graduation night" is a concept I picked up from observing successful school owners from around the country. When I started my first school, I tried to network with and visit as many successful school owners as I could, both to exchange ideas and to observe their "best practices" in action. One thing I observed was that, in many of the most successful schools, they used belt promotions as a means of both increasing their retention and to promote their programs. For retention purposes, nothing beats getting the family members of your students involved and giving them an opportunity to see their loved one in action.

In addition, this is also a powerful incentive for your students to perform well and stay committed to their training. That's because they want to be able to "show" their family how they are progressing in their martial arts training. Graduation night provides them with just such an opportunity.

Likewise when it comes to attracting new students, there are few things more powerful than third-party endorsements. And, the best third-party endorsements are those people can witness with their own eyes. As they say, "Seeing is believing". Well, when friends of your students see them getting recognition for their hard work, and enjoying doing their martial art, it is a powerful recruiting tool for your school.

Holding regular scheduled graduation celebration events where students are ENCOURAGED to invite their friends is a great way to achieve all of the above objectives. So, here's how to run them...

Your First Concerns – Space, Scheduling, and Seating

First, figure out a time that is most convenient for family and friends to attend that does not interfere with regular classes. I've found that Friday nights work best for this. That is, except during football season in Texas – the town I taught in was where they filmed "Varsity Blues", and fall football trumped graduation nights forcing me to schedule on Saturdays to avoid having a poor turnout. So, be sure the date and time you pick won't conflict with any major local events.

Next, find a suitable place to hold your graduations. We held a graduation night every third Friday of each month, so anywhere from about a fourth to a third of our active enrollment would graduate at each event. With a school of 180 to 200 students, you can see how this could become problematic when you add in family and friends. So, when we had a large amount of students graduating, we would either split the ceremony or hold it at another location.

For black belt graduations, this was a must. Over time, I found that renting out local school gymnasiums or church halls was an inexpensive and welcome change from the hassle of doing it at our own school. The added space was a great benefit for demos and so forth, and also made our events seem more formal and "official" to the guests.

For seating, I just went to a local rental store and rented enough metal chairs for all the guests. Total cost on chair and facility rental would typically be around $200 if I did my homework and shopped around. And, it was worth it to spend this much, as you'll see before the end of this article.

RUNNING THE EVENT SMOOTHLY

It helps to have the event itinerary written down well in advance, so you can plan out your entire event schedule and keep things on track. If the event runs longer than 50 minutes, you are going to have a lot of unhappy people on hand. So, keep things running fast with zero downtime, just like in your kids classes.

A good rule of thumb is to do a student demo, an instructor demo, special presentations, then the belt promotion ceremony at the end. You can end with refreshments if you like, but this can be messy if you're hosting it in your own school.

At any rate, here's an example of a typical graduation night event itinerary for your convenience, along with some tips explaining things I've learned over the years about how to run a fun and entertaining grad night event.

Graduation Night Itinerary

5:00 PM – Start setting up. Set up chairs for parents and guests and rope off this area from the training/demo floor.

6:30 PM – Guests and students start showing up.

6:45 PM – Start lining up kids in front and seating them in rows grouped according to age and rank. Have them sit on the floor – it's easier and requires less chairs.

7:00 PM – Kick off the show with a quick introduction and welcome to all the guest and parents. Say something to build up the students... talk about all the hard work that has gone into their training to reach this point. Explain how martial arts is more than just kicks and punches. Share a touching story about how martial arts has helped one of your students. Remember, you have to sell it... you already believe it, but they don't yet. This is public relations for your school – use this opportunity wisely. Also, remember to keep it short so you don't lose the audience's attention.

7:05 PM – Bow the students in and do a group demo of the youngest and newest students. You want them focused and to get their demo out of the way first... everything that comes after should keep them entertained.

7:10 PM – First advanced student or black belt demo.

7:15 PM – Intermediate students group demo.

7:20 PM – Second advanced student or black belt demo.

7:25 PM – Advanced students group demo.

7:30 PM – Master instructor demo. This is your opportunity to show the parents, students, and family members what they never get to see in class – you doing "your thing" whatever that may be. You know you have something you specialize in, so show that. Don't make the mistake of doing things you aren't good at because you think it will please the crowd, because the last thing you need is to give a lackluster performance. For me it was always breaking, but one time I tried to do weapons I wasn't really familiar with and bombed it. Don't make that mistake. Showmanship is key here. Build suspense, be entertaining, and have a good time. Finally, don't take yourself too seriously, no one likes a big head. Be humble and let your skills speak for themselves.

7:40 PM – Color belt promotions. Call the kids up one at a time, have them bow and present their belts. Instruct them to line back up and to place their belts on the floor in front of them, and not to touch them until you instruct them to do so. Once all the belts are passed out, call parents or family members up for each kid and have them assist in tying on the new belts, explaining that it takes the support of family and loved ones for the students to be able to reach this goal. At the end, have them bow, first to you and then to their parents. This is important, it shows you care about the students holistically and not just as a paycheck. Be sincere.

7:45 – Black belt promotions - Make it special if you have black belts to promote. Make sure you tie on their black belts personally! Present them with their certificates, and make sure you instruct them in what it means to be a black belt in front of everyone. This is just as much to teach the crowd as it is for the students being promoted. Remember, you are sharing your value system with these people, something they will likely never be exposed to otherwise. Be brief, be sincere, and be poignant. Your words will last in their minds, trust me.

7:50 – Time to eat cake!

The Best Sort of Advertising Your School Can Have...

All in all, a good graduation night event will serve to make your newer and younger students motivated to reach black belt, to keep your older and more advanced students involved and invested in the school, and it will help make your students' family members and guests feel like they are part of the school as well. In addition, it is a phenomenal opportunity to show a side of your school that people rarely get to see, and to do so in front of people who would never come into your school or classes otherwise.

This ends up being a fantastic recruiting tool. People will start to talk about your graduation events. It will get shared on Facebook and

Tweeted on Twitter. Grandparents and parents will post pictures on their online profiles. People will find out about your school from those who are involved in some way with the promotion event.

This is absolutely the best sort of word-of-mouth advertising your school can have... "buzz" advertising. So, do your very best to make each graduation event fun, entertaining, and inclusive. You WILL reap the rewards from all the hard work you put into it. Try it and see for yourself.

[11]

The Bottom Line

WHAT HAPPENS WHEN YOU IMPLEMENT EVERY STEP

Let's say you have a school of 100 students paying $100/month. Let's also assume that in a single month, you typically enroll ten new students.

- By offering family memberships, you get an additional 3 new students a month at an average of $75 a month = $225.
- You get 5 new referrals from VIP passes and 4 of them enroll... $400 in tuition, not including registration fees.
- You get 2 new students who were shopping around and liked what they saw in your website video... $200 in tuition.
- You reactivate a former student... $100 tuition.

That's ten new students you wouldn't have enrolled otherwise. So far, you've doubled your enrollments with your efforts.

- But wait... you decide to raise your rates from $100 to $129 a month for new students coming in... that's $580 in extra tuition on those 20 new students you enrolled.
- And, one of those students took your discount, enrolled on a three-year program in order to save 20% in their tuition, and paid you a lump sum of $3,700... since you increased your en-

rollments by 10 this month, that's really $3,600 in found money this month... (geez, what if you did that every month?)

- You also had a Pro Shop sale on a new t-shirt design that made you $9 profit on 50 shirts... $450 extra profit.
- You also hosted a Parent's Night Out event that cost you $100 to host, and it made you $650 in profit.
- You start holding graduation ceremonies the last Friday of every month, inviting the parents and families in to watch the students get promoted, and decided to start charging $20 for the new belt and promotion. That's about 25% of your students who test each month, at $16 profit per head... $400 additional profit per month.

THE GRAND TOTAL?

So, that's $6,605.00 in additional profit from implementing all the above strategies in a single month... or, an extra $79,260 in yearly revenue - an 80% increase in gross profit (and almost that in net, since all the above didn't cost you hardly anything to do), and that's not extrapolating for the overall increase in enrollments that should occur from the increase in monthly enrollments.

So, is it worth your time to start implementing all these profit-boosting steps?

I think we both know the answer to that.

[+]

Special Bonus Section

THE TOP 10 MOST IMPORTANT ACTION STEPS YOU MUST TAKE IN PLANNING AND OPENING YOUR MARTIAL ARTS SCHOOL TO ENSURE YOUR SUCCESS IN GOOD TIMES AND BAD...

For the last several years I've been helping martial arts instructors start and grow their martial arts schools, both through the information in my manual and via the articles and reports I've published on my websites and in my newsletter.

On a regular basis, school owners who are in real, serious financial trouble contact me for help. Nearly every month, I get an email that goes something like this:

"If I don't increase my enrollment by next month, I am going to have to shut down my school. I have been paying the rent out of my own pocket, my credit cards are maxed out, and I've cashed out my 401(k) and spent all my savings on keeping this place alive... Can you please give me some guidance or suggestions on how I can save my school?"

It's heart breaking, really it is. And the saddest thing of all is that, in many of these cases, the owners have waited too long to start turning around their business so by the time they contact me it's already too late.

Well, that's why I've provided you with this free report... so YOU don't end up being the next person who contacts me asking for a bucket to bail out your own sinking Titanic of a school. By reading this report, you'll be wise already to the pitfalls and common mistakes new school owners typically make that can spell disaster for their businesses.

So, let's get started...

ACTION STEP #1: "MAKE SURE YOU CAN PAY YOUR EXPENSES BEFORE YOU OPEN YOUR DOORS"

Now, I know this sounds like a no-brainer, but you'd be surprised how many instructors think they can just open their doors and have students come running. Most of these folks have read some story in one of the industry magazines about how Master So-and-so did a grand opening event and opened his doors with 75 students pre-registered for classes.

What they didn't mention in the article was that Master So-and-so already had students in place for months before he opened that location... all those students didn't just magically appear and enroll in one day. And when I say "students in place", what I mean is that the instructor was already teaching part-time programs in the area. So, he or she had a built-in clientele in the area before they went and leased a commercial location.

Now, let's look at the flipside of this by examining the alternative. Calling it "the alternative" is actually a misnomer, considering that it's the way most people start a small business, and it's also the way most entrepreneurial and business programs at colleges and universities teach their students how to start a business. It's also the dumbest and riskiest way to launch a small business, in my opinion and experience.

What's this "risky alternative"? It's getting a loan to finance your studio, which is my opinion is putting the cart before the horse. Here's why; no matter how much research you do, no matter how much demographic information you mine, no matter how good an area looks... you still won't know if your school is going to fly until you open your doors.

I found this out the hard way when I opened my second studio. I started out cocky, and opened it with zero students using my own funds to finance it, which is about 50% in line with the *Small Dojo Big Profits* approach.

Everything went fine for the first year, because I had chosen a very low-overhead location, and kept my expenses to a minimum. Despite opening my doors with no students, I was still in the black (making profit) at the end of the second month. But remember, I was able to get away with doing things that way because I have an education (in business management) and experience (at that time a decade starting and running a successful school from scratch) that most martial arts instructors don't have. But, my overconfidence was nearly my undoing...

Fast-forward to 12 months later. By this time my classes are growing due to the marketing plan I put in place when I first opened, my location, and the reputation I had carefully built in the community (remember, I opened this studio in a town where I knew no one, so I worked hard to meet people in the community and become known). So, I decided to expand in order to add several programs that required more square footage. I also wanted more parking and a more visible location. It so happened that a local women's fitness center was closing, so I jumped on the space. I also took out a loan from my bank on a line of credit, banking on the "fact" that I'd be able to easily pay the increased overhead (more square footage and a prime location on a major thoroughfare with tons of drive-by traffic) with all the fat cash I'd be making from the new programs.

Then, gas prices skyrocketed and the mortgage crisis hit, followed by the worst recession this country has seen since the Great Depression. And, it just so happened that the community I'd chosen to start my studio in (chosen because at the time it was one of the fastest growing areas in Texas) was one of the hardest hit by the mortgage crisis and subsequent fallout. I soon found that carrying that huge (for me) rent and paying those loans was a real burden, since my financial projections didn't account for a massive recession to hit.

The bottom line? I should have waited to expand and financed any expansion out of my own profits, instead of jumping the gun on a "sure thing" and borrowing the money to do it. Sure, I survived and that school ended up becoming a very profitable enterprise, but I also had a lot of sleepless nights getting it to that point. If I had only been patient and more conservative in my business stratagem, I would have dodged that bullet. Lesson learned.

This is one of the most important things I show you how to do in *Small Dojo Big Profits*; that is, how to open your doors with enough students to pay your expenses from day one. And, I also show you how to grow your school without needing outside financing, as well as how to keep your profit margins exceedingly high so your risk is minimal. It takes more time and effort than signing a loan, sure... but in this economic climate, you definitely need to mitigate your risk.

Bottom line? Don't go open a studio in a new location with zero students and expect to go from scratch to profit in 30 days – it just isn't going to happen. Instead, build your clientele in an area first, and then once you have enough paying students to cover your bills, you can open your doors knowing you're already in profit.

Action Step #2: "Keep Your Expenses Low and Your Profits High"

So, how do you do this? There's a whole laundry list of things you need to know to keep your expenses and overhead to an absolute bare minimum, but the number one place new school owners screw up is on their rent.

More specifically, they get a whole heck of a lot more space than they really need and then can't make their rent. You might think that having a whole heck of a lot of space would be just peachy, but remember that you don't need *more* than a few thousand square feet to operate a thriving studio. Getting all that extra space is just going to put you in the hole before you even have a ladder to climb out on.

Think back to what I just told you about my decision to expand my second studio. I really didn't need the extra space I was getting, and I *really* didn't need the massive increase in rent for that pretty storefront location either. I was doing just fine in my original small, slightly cramped but still serviceable low-overhead location.

I know, I know; the conventional wisdom in the industry is that you need a storefront location with plenty of foot traffic in order to be financially successful. I say "baloney." In fact, some of the most profitable martial arts studios I've seen (including my own) have been in horrible locations.

I'm talking small, postage-stamp sized studios in out-of-the way, inconvenient locations (but there's an art to doing this, so don't think you can open a school in the middle of nowhere and succeed, it doesn't work like that). Second-floor spaces, spaces tucked way in the back of shopping centers, spaces with absolutely no storefront or street exposure (my first studio was just such a location), and so on.

And what's the one thing all these locations have in common? Low rent! In fact, I've seen school owners do exceptionally well in these locations, in many different instances over the years.

So, keep your overhead low, starting with your rent and working out from there.

ACTION STEP #3: "DON'T GET CAUGHT UP CHASING THE 'BIG SCHOOL DREAM'"

In *Small Dojo Big Profits* I explain why chasing that big school dream isn't always the wisest business decision, and how it can actually hinder your chances of success when you are just starting out. Case in point: the successes, near-failures, and failures of people I've guided through the process of starting their own martial arts schools.

I've personally coached a few of my close friends as they opened studios that got off the ground successfully because they listened to me and didn't get too extravagant on how much space they rented. The result was that they were able to handle their expenses and manage their workload even in the early start-up phase of their studios.

However, as the saying goes familiarity breeds contempt. Inevitably after a while my friends started reading those industry magazines and got stars in their eyes reading articles about Master So-and-so's 10,000 sq. ft. school. After they read about how he or she has 800 students all training in the same location, suddenly Mike's advice is just holding them back, and the wheels start turning inside their heads. *"Man, screw Mike and his small school business system. I want to have a school with 800 students, and I'm going to need a place to put them, too."* *Sigh*

Not only is this in violation of action step #2 above, it's putting the cart before the horse as well as running the wrong race to boot. In one instance it resulted in my friend eventually losing his formerly highly profitable school when the economy slowed down and his enrollments plummeted. In another instance, my friends nearly had to close their doors after a second location (another high-disaster-potential approach to growing your martial arts school operation is running a multi-school operation) became a huge financial drain on their business.

Listen... your first priority in building your school is to get to 100 students in the shortest period of time possible. Then, your next step is to build your enrollment to 150 – 175 students. After you've run a school of that size successfully for a year or two, then you can start thinking about what type of lifestyle you'd like to lead, and whether it's worth it to sacrifice all your time (and in many cases, most of your profit) just to be able to say you have 500 or 1,000 students and a school that's the size of most Globo Gyms.

But until then, don't even think about opening a second location or expanding your square footage, because you don't need it, and you likely don't have the skills or experience to be able to do it successfully anyhow. Stay small and you'll stay profitable, even when the economy tanks; believe me, I'm speaking from experience.

ACTION STEP #4: "IT'S A BUSINESS, NOT A HOBBY – TREAT IT LIKE ONE"

Right now, you probably are not teaching full-time or earning your full-time income from teaching martial arts. So, you most likely have a job that you have to go to for a certain number of hours each day, and you have to do a certain amount of work and produce a certain level of productivity in order to keep your job and continue to receive a paycheck each month. Am I right?

So, answer me this: Why is it that people think things will be any different when they start a small business?

If you think opening a school will mean that you get to take vacation every month, or that you get to take sick days whenever you want, or that the only time you'll have to work is when you're teaching classes, you are sadly mistaken. It may shock and amaze you to find that most entrepreneurs work twice as hard and have to be twice as productive in their workweek as the average wage earner, because that's precisely what it takes to successfully launch and run a small business.

Sure, the rewards are exponentially greater, but that's the payoff you get for being willing to work your tail off and take a major financial risk in starting a small business. If you want to reap the rewards of small business ownership then you need to be willing to put in twice the work and achieve twice the productivity that you do in your job now. (And incidentally, anyone who says "You didn't build that" has obviously never started and operated a small business, because they have no idea how much work goes into small business ownership.)

You must set regular hours for your business and stick to them if you want to succeed. Sure, at first when you're still working your day job, those hours may only be 5pm to 9 pm Monday through Friday, and 9am to noon on Saturday. But, you need to advertise those hours and stick to them. Also, you need to accept that even though your business is only open for "part-time" hours, you need to work in it full-time... regardless of any other job responsibilities you may have.

When I hear someone whining about how they have to work all day long and then go straight to their studio to work another four hours, I get really irate. Why? Because when I launched my first studio, I worked ten hours shifts with a 30 minute commute. I got up at zero-dark-thirty every morning to get to a job that I chose because it didn't interfere with my hours of operation, worked for ten hours, and then I drove straight to the studio to teach for three or four hours and stay after to do the books and plan out my next day. And I was *happy* to do it.

Why was I happy to be working my tail off and burning the candle at both ends? For several reasons:

1. I was finally getting paid to do what I love.

2. I was building a business that I built with my own two hands, and that's incredibly satisfying.

3. I saw the light at the end of the tunnel. I knew I wasn't going to be working for slave wages much longer.

4. Who complains that they have deeply satisfying and reasonably well-paying work to do? (I'll tell you who; a lazy ingrate with a sense of entitlement and a skewed sense of what's "fair", that's who. Don't count yourself among that lot if you want to be a success in business.)

5. I knew what it was like to go hungry, I knew what it was like to scrape by on slave wages, and I knew what it was like to go without. I also knew that few people are able to get paid for doing what they love, and I counted myself blessed everyday to have the opportunity to build a business that would allow me to do exactly that (see items one through four above).

Besides, there is nothing in the world that feels as good as telling your boss he or she can kiss your rear goodbye. Not only that, but every bit of extra work and "overtime" you put into your own business is directly increasing your own paycheck. The long hours you work during the first year or so while you're getting your business off the ground are a pittance in trade for the personal satisfaction of knowing you are the captain of your own vessel.

Trust me, it's well worth it.

ACTION STEP #5: "ACCEPT IT - YOU ARE IN THE BUSINESS OF ATTRACTING NEW BUSINESS!"

From the moment you put pen to paper on your business plan, you are in the business of attracting new business. Every day in your small business, you will wear many hats, but none are so important as the hat that reads, "professional marketer." And, failure to accept this oh-so-vital fact of life as a business owner has tanked many a small business.

I've seen it happen time and again as I've coached martial arts school owners over the last decade or so. For whatever reason, school owners decide that their number one job is teaching (an easy mistake to make), or customer service (your number two job, actually), or writing lesson plans, or hosting seminars, or coaching a winning competition team, or getting manifold certifications in multiple martial arts systems, or (my favorite) training in martial arts.

Wrong! Your number one job is marketing, period, end of discussion! And that's because if the phone doesn't ring, and if you aren't enrolling enough new students each and every month to increase your enrollment and replace the students you are going to lose no matter what, then it's just a short matter of time before your doors close.

I've personally witnessed thriving martial arts studios shrink down to nothing and even close after being sold to extremely talented and knowledgeable instructors who thought their number one job was teaching martial arts. In one case, the new owner was a much more knowledgeable instructor than the first owner; in another, the second owner was better fighter.

Yet, in both cases the original owner knew something that the subsequent owners didn't; that is, *marketing is the lifeblood of a successful martial arts school.* Not curriculum, not competition, not seminars, not rank and certifications, not the qualifications of the instructors; no it's marketing and getting new business. Certainly, all those things matter, but nothing matters so much as that you are constantly drumming up new business for your studio.

It's true; when you open the doors on your new school, you are officially in the marketing business. Your number one, numero uno job at that point is not to teach classes... oh no-no-no. Instead, it's to increase your revenue by marketing and selling your services.

This one is important. Tattoo it inside your eyelids. You'll thank me for it later.

ACTION STEP #6: "LEARN HOW TO MARKET NOW - BEFORE YOU OPEN YOUR DOORS"

Waiting to learn how to market your services until after you open your doors is like going on a safari and waiting to buy a gun until that Cape buffalo is about to run you down. Seriously, it is just like that. No one hunts dangerous game without first buying a firearm and heading to the range to sight that thing in and practice putting a round in the ten ring. Likewise, no one should open a business without first getting their hands on a ton of small business marketing material and studying it until their eyes bug out.

Think about it - if marketing really is the lifeblood of your business, then you had better become an expert at marketing before you open your doors! Just looking at a few articles about how someone grew their martial art school using school talks isn't enough. Printing up your business cards and planning a ribbon-cutting ceremony with the local chamber isn't enough. Just putting up a free website using a free web hosting service isn't enough. And, just printing up some glossy brochures to put on your front counter *certainly* isn't enough (and if you think brochures sell lessons, you're screwed already).

Nope... you need to know every aspect of marketing, including which marketing methods are most effective for your industry, how to craft an ad and write sales copy that sells, what offers are tested to work most effectively for your market, how to craft an offer that gets people to respond, what NOT to put in an ad or marketing piece, who your target market is and where to find them, how to create a marketing plan... I could go on and on.

Certainly, you can't just become a marketing expert overnight, which is why you need to start learning how to market your school long before you first open your doors. This is another reason why I recommend building a clientele before you lease a commercial location. Doing so allows you to start honing your marketing skills in real time, but without the pressure of knowing that if your marketing campaigns don't work it could mean you have to shut your doors.

So start learning how to market NOW before you open your doors. Read everything you can on small business marketing, then read some more. FYI, most of the information written on how to market your martial art school is junk. Purchase and study my martial arts marketing system first (MartialArtsMarketingBook.com), and then read some of the *Guerilla Marketing* books and Bob Bly's *Copywriting Handbook* to round out the foundation of your marketing skill set.

ACTION STEP #7: "USE CONTRACTS - ETHICALLY"

Look, people are fickle. I don't care how great an instructor you are, or how much your students love you, they are going to do whatever they think benefits them and their family the most at any given time. That's why you need to get people to commit with more than just their word and good intentions when they enroll.

There are a few reasons why people tend to renege on their agreements, and it's important to understand them. By understanding human nature we can then see why it's so important that we be crystal clear about and absolutely firm on our membership policies.

REASON #1: FAMILIARITY BREEDS CONTEMPT

People tend to show the most respect and courtesy people they don't know, and they tend to be reserved in social situations where they are unfamiliar with others around them. However, people also tend to be more willing to take advantage of those people they know best, because it's easy to take someone for granted when you are in close contact with them every day.

Think about it. Your neighbor has no problem borrowing your hedge trimmers and keeping them all winter. The girl in the cubicle next to you at work is fine with eating your lunch from the fridge in the break room. And, your best friend is okay with borrowing a ten spot from you for drinks which he knows he will probably never pay back to you.

So, it's no surprise that this tendency transfers to the student-teacher relationship...*especially when you get overly chummy with your clients.*

Reason #2: Many People Today Practice Elastic Ethics Based on Peer Opinions

It's actually become a cultural phenomenon that people today operate ethically and morally based more on their feelings than on firm ethical guidelines and logic. Even more compelling is the tendency to take on "social group ethics", where the generally accepted social mores of the individual's peer group take precedence over their own internal moral compass. In other words, when faced with a moral dilemma, the tendency today is to poll the peer group and go with the general consensus. You will lose that contest, every single time as a business owner.

Just look around you. We've moved from a society with clear moral and ethical guidelines and expectations, to that of one where if you don't feel like doing something, *or if your friends think it's bogus*, then that *must* mean you shouldn't do it... even when you've already signed a written agreement or given your word that you would.

Reason #3: People Tend to Look Out for Number One

Face it, your clients could care less if you have bills to pay. They don't spend two seconds a day wondering if you have money for groceries, or to send your kids to college, or to sock away for retirement. In short, when they're not in class they're not thinking about you at all.

Look, your clients could care less about your financial future... because they are too busy attending to their own. So, accept this and get over it. Then, come to the understanding that it's up to you to look out for your current and future financial well-being, because no one else is going to do it for you.

Reason #4: People Tend To Take the Path of Least Resistance

This is purely human nature; always has been, always will be. And if that means the pain of losing face due to reneging on a contractual agreement with their instructor is less than the pain of the consequences, *they are going to cancel that agreement every single time.*

So, clients are going to cancel on you based on what path is less painful... which is why you need to be absolutely firm on your contractual policies and the consequences of breaking your contract. Give your students plenty of time to try out your services at no obligation, and let them know they are making a commitment of time and money to join your school. Then, make them commit to training at your school for a specified period of time.

Those who balk at signing up for a basic membership of six months to a year probably aren't going to stick around anyway, and they are not your ideal clients. Use your membership agreement to weed out the tire kickers and ensure your ongoing, continued financial stability and cash flow.

Action Step #8: "Maintain Complete Control of Your Own Finances and Cash Flow... in Other Words, Be Your Own Billing Company"

Sometimes it's best to outsource a task in order to improve efficiency and increase productivity in your business. However, your martial arts tuition collection is one case where it's actually better to do it yourself.

For starters, it doesn't take you any more time to do. You have to fill out the same paperwork, regardless of who handles the payment processing. And, it only takes a minute or so to enter the billing information into your payment gateway... but that extra minute of work can save you thousands over time.

The best part is, it cuts out the middle man (the billing company), potentially saving you tens of thousands of dollars in billing fees. All you pay is the processing fee for the payment – typically 1 – 3 % for credit cards, and a flat fee of .25 to .50 cents per transaction for debit card and electronic check processing. Your online payment gateway should be around $10 a month, and the merchant credit card processing company usually also charges a fee of $10 a month for sending you a statement (I know, it's lame, but it's an accepted practice in the industry).

I figure that I've saved at least $4,000 a year since I started doing my own billing this way in-house. And, the best part is that by billing everyone electronically, my on-time collections actually increased from 75% to over 95% when compared to using the billing company to handle my collections for me.

But wait... won't this make you "the bad guy" with your students if you have to take their money every month? Give me a break – that's a myth that was created by the martial arts billing companies as a way to sell you on their over-priced services. Their argument was that, when you had to call students to remind them to pay their tuition, you'd become "the bad guy" and they'd stop coming to classes.

Well, I'm here to tell you that's a load of bull. Here's why:

For one, billing everyone electronically virtually eliminates late payments. So, *it's rare that you have to call students regarding late payments.*

Second, *on the odd occasion when you do have to call a student to find out why their payment didn't come through,* you can actually take the position of being the GOOD guy: "Hi Mrs. Jones, this is Mr. Smith over at Smith's Martial Arts. I noticed your payment didn't go through and I was just calling to see if your debit card may have expired. I wanted to correct it before the late fees kick in so you don't have to pay an additional fee." See? You're actually trying to help the client out.

Third, *if someone doesn't want to pay you their tuition,* no amount of phone calls and late notice letters are going to make them pay.

Virtually every billing company I ever used had a "collections department." And, in all the years I used those over-priced billing companies, do you want to know how many times they actually collected on my delinquent accounts? Care to guess? That's right... zero, nada, zilch, never.

So, don't buy into that load of bull about being the bad guy. Honest students know they have to pay you, and they know you have to collect your tuition to make a living. Feeling bad about getting your money is just one step away from feeling guilty about making a living teaching martial arts. *Don't fall into that trap.*

On the other hand, paying someone 7-10% of your gross revenues just for the privilege of collecting your own money for you is just plain stupid... especially when there are a ton of alternative billing methods available to you these days. Instead, set up EFT's through your bank for automated check payments and get your credit card company to set up an online payment gateway for you.

The online payment gateway will allow you to set up automated recurring billing on your clients' debit and credit cards and even on their checking accounts for an additional monthly fee. It's much cheaper, you'll actually collect more payments on time than a billing company will, you'll get your money faster, and you won't lose students due to poor billing company service and rude collection phone calls when they are late.

ACTION STEP #9: "PROVIDE THE TYPE OF CUSTOMER SERVICE THAT CAUSES YOUR STUDENTS TO *WANT* TO REFER THEIR FRIENDS AND FAMILY TO YOUR SCHOOL"

This doesn't mean you have to bend over backwards and kiss everyone's rump... that'll just spoil your students and then they'll be walking all over you. What I'm talking about is making sure you deliver on your promises (better grades and attitude for kids, learning self-defense and getting in shape for adults) every single day.

Many instructors make the mistake of assuming that students are loyal forever, no matter how they're treated. So, they think they're free to over-charge and under-deliver, to miss classes regularly, to show up late and unprepared, and to simply be a really cruddy instructor. They think, "Sure, students may complain, but where else are they going to go for lessons?" I can tell you where, right down the street to your competition.

Many years ago when I started training in the martial arts, customer service was definitely not a closely examined issue. You paid your tuition, attended class, practiced at home, and that was enough. From the student's perspective, as long as the school was open and classes were held as scheduled, all was well. And, from the instructor's perspective as long as the students paid tuition on time and showed up for class, he or she was satisfied with the arrangement.

However, for better or for worse the industry has changed considerably since those days. Now, martial arts business and management is heavily influenced by fitness industry practices that have been adopted by our industry... practices which often seem to value profit over people.

Unfortunately, we seem to have integrated some of the very worst fitness industry practices right along with some of the best. And along the way, common-sense "golden rule" customer service and relations has gone straight out the window in many schools.

As I recently wrote on my blog, we have entered the age of the consumer. Consumers today are smarter, better informed, much less trusting, in some ways much more demanding, and they have quite a bit of power to influence public perception of your business for good or ill. So, it's almost obligatory in today's society to take customer service seriously.

For this reason (and also because it's the right thing to do), you need to be professional, keep your school neat and clean, show up to work every day, on time and ready to perform at your peak for the entire day. Teach each class like it's your last chance to keep your students... because it is. Treat every student like you'd want to be treated – learn everyone's name, and send cards and thank you notes regularly.

Always be one step ahead of your competition, do more and be simply better than anyone else in your community. That's how you turn students into raving fans.

ACTION STEP #10: "ABP – ALWAYS BE PROMOTING"

Since your number one job is marketing your school, you need to have the mindset that you should always be promoting your business. Once you internalize this attitude, you'll soon begin to see multiple new opportunities for promoting your business each and every day. Your doing so needs to become a habit, something that's a regular part of every moment of every day.

Here are just a few examples:

✓ Hand out business cards at every opportunity

✓ Speak and make appearances whenever possible

✓ Get out and meet people in your community, and let them know what you do

✓ Take an influential person in your community to lunch at least once a month, ask questions and listen to their answers, then find a way to help them that also helps you · Donate to and support charitable causes in your community

✓ Put signage on your vehicles and keep them neat and clean

✓ Wear your school t-shirts around town with your logo clearly visible on the front and back and get your students to do the same

✓ Sell school window decals, or provide them for free

✓ Build a great marketing website and place the address on everything

✓ Ask your students for referrals at least once a month.

Always be promoting!

For Sample Forms and Documents

For access to my entire archive of sample martial arts school management forms and documents, including:

- Waiver forms
- Membership agreements
- Class schedules
- Ads and marketing documents
- Event fliers
- Staff and hiring documents
- Program description handouts
- And much more...

...then visit **MartialArtSchoolAlliance.com** and sign-up for the trial membership. By doing so you'll have access to all the documents, forms, and content on the site at a very minimal cost.

More Books By Mike Massie

For more books by Mike Massie on achieiving martial arts business success, visit his author page at:

Amazon.com/author/mikemassie

MY OTHER MARTIAL ARTS BUSINESS BOOKS:

- *Small Dojo Big Profits: A Complete Guide to Starting and Running a Highly Profitable Martial Arts School*
- *Martial Arts Character Education Lesson Plans for Children*
- *Developing Staff and Leadership Teams - How to Run and Grow Your Martial Arts School Efficiently With Minimal Staff and Payroll Overhead*
- *Martial Arts Drills and Games for Kids (Drills and Games Vol I)*
- *MMA, Grappling, and Self-Defense Drills and Warm-Ups (Drills and Games Vol II)*
- *How to Teach Using a Rotating Curriculum in Your Karate School*
- *The Best of Martial Arts Business Daily*
- *The Best of Starting a Martial Art School*
- *The Top 10 Most Important Action Steps for Starting a Martial Art School That Will Thrive Through Good Times and Bad* (full text included in this book)

Index

About the Author

Mike Massie is the author of *Small Dojo Big Profits* and has been a professional martial arts instructor for over twenty years. Mr. Massie holds dan ranks in Sil Jeon Mu Sul, Moo Duk Kwan, Tae Kwon Do, Hapkido, Shotokan, and Jujutsu, and has been studying and training in the martial arts since 1984.

Mr. Massie graduated from St. Edward's University in 2004 with a Bachelor's degree in Allied Health Science and a Minor in Business Administration. He is the creator of Fighting Fit Boot Camp and The Self Defense Black Belt Program. He is also a certified personal fitness trainer with the National Exercise and Sports Trainers Association (lifetime) and a certified kettlebell coach.

Through his materials, including his manuals, articles, websites, blog, and newsletter, Mr. Massie has helped thousands of martial arts instructors achieve greater financial success, while finding increased personal satisfaction in their careers as professional martial artists.

Mr. Massie lives with his family in Austin, Texas.

42367238R00087

Made in the USA
Lexington, KY
18 June 2015